W9-AHJ-938

Georgia
CURIOSITIES

Help Us Keep This Guide Up to Date

Every effort has been made by the author and editors to make this guide as accurate and useful as possible. However, many things can change after a guide is published—establishments close, phone numbers change, hiking trails are rerouted, facilities come under new management, etc.

We would love to hear from you concerning your experiences with this guide and how you feel it could be made better and be kept up to date. While we may not be able to respond to all comments and suggestions, we'll take them to heart and we'll also make certain to share them with the author. Please send your comments and suggestions to the following address:

The Globe Pequot Press
Reader Response/Editorial Department
P.O. Box 480
Guilford, CT 06437

Or you may e-mail us at:

editorial@GlobePequot.com

Thanks for your input, and happy travels!

Georgia CURIOSITIES

QUIRKY CHARACTERS, ROADSIDE ODDITIES & OTHER OFFBEAT STUFF

WILLIAM SCHEMMEL

SECOND EDITION

INSIDERS' GUIDE®

GUILFORD, CONNECTICUT
AN IMPRINT OF THE GLOBE PEQUOT PRESS

OAK BROOK PUBLIC LIBRARY
600 OAK BROOK ROAD
OAK BROOK, IL 60523

To buy books in quantity for corporate use
or incentives, call **(800) 962–0973,**
or e-mail **premiums@GlobePequot.com.**

INSIDERS' GUIDE ®

Copyright © 2007 by Morris Book Publishing, LLC

All rights reserved. No part of this book may be reproduced or transmitted in any form by any means, electronic or mechanical, including photocopying and recording, or by any information storage and retrieval system, except as may be expressly permitted by the 1976 Copyright Act or by the publisher. Requests for permission should be made in writing to The Globe Pequot Press, P.O. Box 480, Guilford, Connecticut 06437.

Insiders' Guide is a registered trademark of Morris Book Publishing, LLC.

Text design by Nancy Freeborn
Layout by Debbie Nicolais
Maps by Rusty Nelson © Morris Book Publishing, LLC
Interior photos by the author, except the following: p. 128: Marietta Welcome Center and Visitors Bureau; p. 148: the Augusta Canal Authority; p. 189: Booth Western Art Museum; and p. 271: Chandler Goff.

ISSN 1542-1252
ISBN-13: 978-0-7627-4110-6
ISBN-10: 0-7627-4110-4

Manufactured in the United States of America
Second Edition/First Printing

To Roscoe, my faithful companion these many years.

Acknowledgments

A "Thank You" as big as Georgia to the dedicated regional representatives of the Georgia Department of Industry, Trade and Tourism: Becky Basset, Cheryl Smith, Jeannie Buttrum, Mary Jo Dudley, Becky Morris, and Kitty Sikes; also, Lisa Love, with the Macon-Bibb County Convention and Visitors Bureau; Rebecca Rogers with the Augusta Canal Authority; Shelby Guest with the Columbus CVB; Hannah Smith with the Athens CVB; and members of local tourism boards all over the state, who directed me to so many wonderful curiosities. I hope you like it!

GEORGIA

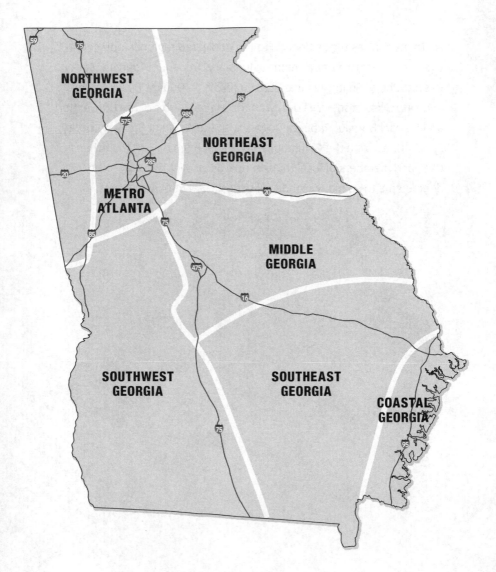

Contents

Introduction

Give it the proverbial lick and a promise, and the Peach State seems as normal as blueberry pie. But peek under the crust and, like Harry Potter's magical world, Georgia brims with curiosities enough to fill a book. Like this one. Look along the roadsides—among the fast-food strips and barbecue joints—and you'll spot totem-size chickens, whopping big rabbits, grinning peanuts, outsize apples, peaches, and pigs. We collect parts of Elvis. Yankees and Canadians think we talk funny. (Know something? Y'all do too, eh!) We eat every part of the pig—sometimes even the squeal—make jelly and candy from an obnoxious Japanese weed, insist on RC Cola with our MoonPies, and drink iced tea so sweet it sets off car alarms.

If you're going to seriously seek out Georgia's curiosities, be sure you've got a reliable ride, a lot of time, and infinite patience. A trustworthy road map and a sense of humor (and the absurd) are also essential. We're the biggest state this side of the Mississippi—almost 400 miles long from Lookout Mountain on the top to Valdosta way down on the bottom, and more than 250 miles from Savannah on the Atlantic to Columbus on the Chattahoochee River. It seems all the bigger because so much of it seems so empty. Half of the 9.1 million Georgians are tied up in a Gordian knot around Atlanta. The second-tier cities—Augusta, Macon, Columbus, Savannah—come in with about 250,000 residents each, and many county-seat towns have barely enough folks to form a good line at the Dairy Queen. So there's plenty of elbow room and lots of out-of-the-way places to explore.

Let's start at the top. I'm sorry to say that the Reverend Howard Finster has departed his Paradise Garden for Paradise in another dimension, but the folk artist exalted by the Smithsonian claimed that he had visions of Hitler and Elvis, so don't be surprised if you turn a corner in his hometown of Summerville and see Howard, der Fuehrer, and the King swapping stories on a bench in front of the courthouse. Late at night you might sneak up on the ghosts of Godfrey and Julia at Barnsley gardens, but as far as I've ever heard, Susan Hayward is content in her churchyard plot at Carrollton. Fans of *Midnight in the Garden of Good and Evil* will have to venture way off the trodden path to find shooter Jim Williams's restless spirit in very rural Wilkinson County. Meanwhile, shootee Danny Hansford is trying to finagle his way out of his fancy graveyard in Savannah so that he can get his hands on the man who done him wrong.

If you don't see any ghosts in Savannah, you just aren't looking. Check around the downtown cafeteria line—isn't that Little Gracie picking out a congealed salad? How did that gent in colonial finery vanish from our table so fast? Goodness me, the lady in the old-fashioned dress who was sitting here a second ago sure looks a lot like that portrait over the fireplace.

Except for a few sourpusses, we enjoy a good laugh at ourselves. Flannery O'Connor, Lewis Grizzard, and Erskine Caldwell had a high old time with our peculiarities. The Redneck Games in East Dublin spoof Atlanta's 1996 Olympics with mud-pit wrestling, armpit serenading, and hubcap hurling. We try not to look gift horses in the mouth, but back in 1929 Rome almost forgot its manners when it received a she-wolf suckling her two-legged pups from Benito Mussolini. Henry Ford's largesse was met with far more grace. About half the states in the country have some kind of Elvis museum, but none I've heard of can match Joni Mabe's for-sure royal wart and "maybe" toenail.

You can eat well everywhere in Georgia. If your taste runs to barbecue, have your 'cue and Brunswick stew—and your name on a plywood piggy—at Oscar Poole's Pig Hill of Fame in East Ellijay. Don't dawdle at the 4-Way Lunch in Cartersville and be careful about asking the secret of the sauce at Vienna's Big Pig Jig. Pick up a sackful of Nu-Way Weiners in Macon before hitting the Interstate 16 twilight zone to Savannah. At the Rattlesnake Roundups in Whigham and Claxton, find out for yourselves whether it really does taste like chicken. At Climax Swine Time discover the secret of a superior mess of chitlins—betcha can't eat more than one of Lieutenant Stevens's Scrambled Dogs at the Dinglewood Pharmacy lunch counter in Columbus.

We put a lot of store in our animal friends. Mobs of kangaroos are on the loose in Dawson County. The Big Rabbit waves a big how-do in—where else?—Rabbittown. The Big Chicken directs the lost and forlorn on a Metro Atlanta highway, and Burmese junglefowl run wild in downtown Fitzgerald. A memorial with his image honors Buster the Police Dog, who died in the line of duty. Make sure you secure your pets and your children while admiring the buzzards at Reed Bingham State Park. And if you wonder what 25 million crickets sound like, the answer is at the world's largest cricket farm in Glennville. In need of stress-reducing therapy? Northern Spy is "in" at Melon Bluff on the coast.

Like our neighboring states, we've got our feet planted in the here-and-now, with one eye on then-and-gone. The Confederate Memorial chiseled on Stone Mountain wouldn't be politically or socially possible today, but if you're on the big granite dome on a rainy summer day you might snag a bucket of fairy shrimp from under Bobby Lee's nose. Shell Annie is one of my favorite Civil War stories—it's too good to be true—but Peter Bonner of Historical and Hysterical Tours swears it's gospel, and we all know that tour guides never exaggerate.

Speaking of the "wah," PC or not, Peggy Mitchell's little yarn, and the movie spun from it, are a revered part of our culture. Three metro museums have *Gone With the Wind* Oscars, costumes, and other great stuff. While browsing the Road to Tara Museum in Jonesboro, look for Elvis carrying the Rebel flag in the Confederate mural, and don't miss the macabre accoutrements around the corner in the world's only drive-by

Antique Funeral Home Museum. Before Isidor Strauss made it big as the founder of Macy's and a *Titanic* casualty, he was the overseas agent for a Columbus group financing Confederate ironclads. Forget? Not just yet. A plaque in the Old Capitol in Milledgeville exalts the session that thrust Georgia into the hell of the Civil War. The commandant of the notorious Andersonville POW camp was hanged for war crimes, but a monument across the road from the camp honors him as a hero.

In Athens the world's only double-barreled cannon still aims north "just in case." If it ever does go off, the clumsy old gun might fell the world's only oak tree with a deed to itself. We'll go to great lengths to preserve a revered landmark or heirloom. A sixteenth-century book in the University of Georgia library was bound in human skin. "Save Our Butt" saved a beloved little Augusta bridge from the highway department's greedy grasp, and "Swamp Gravy" charmingly captures the songs and folklore of Colquitt and Miller County, in the southwest corner's peanut and cotton country.

We throw a festival for just about everything. From nature's bounty: apples, azaleas, roses, geraniums, camellias, catfish, crawfish, grits, granite, honeybees, mayhaws, moonshine, mules, onions, peaches, pecans, peanuts, pigs, and shrimp. And if-you-can't-beat-'em-throw-'em-a-party: rattlesnakes, fire ants, kudzu, and buzzards.

Roaming the state, don't miss the Statue of Liberty (McRae), Georgia's Little Grand Canyon (Lumpkin), and our very own Stonehenge (Elbert County). Bring your phrase book when you visit Rome, Milan, Berlin, Cairo, Vienna, Damascus, Sparta, Athens, Scotland, and Quebec. And if you discover any curiosities I've overlooked, be sure to send 'em along, you heah?

SYMBOLICALLY SPEAKING,
GEORGIA'S OFFICIAL SYMBOLS

We're so proud of our state that we've got more than forty "official" ambassadors to spread our message to the world.

• Delegates to the 1951 State Democratic Convention got so giddy when Thomasvillian James Burch played one of his compositions that they returned to the capitol in three-quarter time and declared "Our Georgia" our official state waltz: "It's a grand old state, our Georgia, where the Swanee River flows, a bit of God's heaven, as everybody knows, and when I go roaming, a longing fills my breast, a song there comes from my heart, for the state I love best." Eat your heart out, Strauss.

• The 9.1 million of us are bound by the "Georgians' Creed," adopted in 1939. Raise your right hand and repeat after me: "Accepting as I do the principles upon which Georgia was founded, not for self, but for others; its democratic form of government based on 'Wisdom, Justice, and Moderation'; its natural resources; its educational, social, and religious advantages, making it a most desirable place to live, I will strive to be a pure upright citizen, rejecting evils, loving and emulating the good. I further believe it is my duty to defend it against all enemies, to honor and obey its laws, to apply the Golden Rule in all dealings with my fellow citizens. I feel a sense of pride in the history and heroic deeds accomplished by my forebears and shall endeavor to so live that my state will be proud of me for doing my bit to make my state a better commonwealth for future generations."

- Pogo, who declareth, "We have met the enemy and he is us," is our official possum.

- "Georgia on My Mind" became the official state song by acclamation when Albany native Ray Charles serenaded the legislature in 1979.

- The shark tooth is the official fossil. (What better judges of fossils are there than the gentle ladies and gentlemen of the legislature?)

- "Shoot the Bull," an annual Hawkinsville shindig, is the official beef cook-off.

- Jimmy Carter is twice blessed. Plains High School, Jimmah's alma mater, is the official school; peanuts, the official crop.

We also have official poultry (fried, baked, and potpied); official reptile (gopher tortoise); official pork cook-off (Vienna's Big Pig Jig); official fish (largemouth bass); official mammal (there's a right whale and a . . .); official vegetable (Vidalia Sweet Onion); official fruit (California and South Carolina grow a few more peaches than we do, but ours are extra special; anyway, "Soybean State" and "Chicken State" don't have the same ring as "Peach State"); official game bird (bobwhite quail; millions are blasted in the name of sport every year; for a primer see Tom Wolfe's novel *A Man in Full*). And to tell us how soon spring's going to be here, we have an official weather prognosticator (see "Beau Knows" in the Metro Atlanta chapter).

NORTHEAST GEORGIA

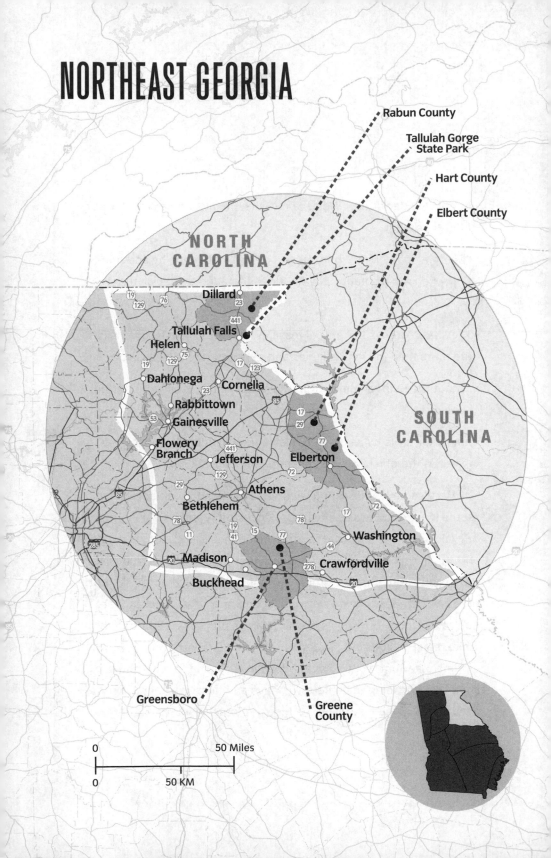

Rabun County

Tallulah Gorge State Park

Hart County

Elbert County

NORTH CAROLINA

SOUTH CAROLINA

Dillard

Tallulah Falls

Helen

Dahlonega

Cornelia

Rabbittown

Gainesville

Flowery Branch

Jefferson

Elberton

Athens

Bethlehem

Washington

Madison

Crawfordville

Buckhead

Greensboro

Greene County

0   50 Miles

0   50 KM

NORTHEAST GEORGIA

Northeast Georgia unfolds in a tapestry of Blue Ridge Mountains, rivers, lakes, and dancing waterfalls. Folded into it are quaint old towns, lively cities, and crossroads villages with nothing more than a country store and a cluster of churches. While you're walking the Appalachian Trail; risking life, limb, and hairdo on the Chattooga River's rapids; or gasping for oxygen on peaks that bump the clouds at more than 4,000 feet, take time to marvel at a wart from Elvis's royal wrist; the Big Red Apple and the Big Rabbit, and a book made of human skin. And there's more! Georgia's take on England's Stonehenge is in a field outside Elberton. "Alpine Helen" brought Bavaria to the Blue Ridge. America's very first gold rush echoed through the hills around Dahlonega. In Athens, Uga is top dog, a tree holds the deed to itself, and a clumsy Civil War cannon points north—"just in case."

The Double-barreled Cannon
Athens

A century before the University of Georgia's hometown became synonymous with Bulldog football, R.E.M., and the B-52s, the Double-barreled Cannon gave Athens a more dubious distinction. Invented by John Gilleland, a homeboy house builder, the big guy rolled out of an Athens foundry in 1863. Advance publicity touted it as the ultimate Yankee-waster. Loaded with two shots connected by a chain, it would sweep across a battlefield like a souped-up scythe and cut down twice as many bluecoats in half the time. Regretfully, when the cannon was test-fired, the joined missiles plowed up an acre of ground, tore up a cornfield, and cut down small trees. Then the chain broke. The rounds flew off in opposite directions, killing a cow, knocking down a log cabin's brick chimney, and sending who knows how many of Athens's fair ladies to their swooning couches. Today the old soldier sits peacefully on City Hall's lawn, pointing north— just in case.

The Double-barreled Cannon's 1863 rollout was a big, loud dud, but the big guy is waiting patiently on the Athens City Hall lawn, just in case the Yankees or UGA football foes get into range.

The Tree That Owns Itself

Athens

Woodsman, spare that tree! The majestic white oak (*Quercus alba*) towering proud and tall over the corner of Dearing and Finley Streets, holds its fate in its own huge leafy arms. It's been so since 1890, when Colonel W. H. Jackson, a University of Georgia professor, repaid the tree for its many years of loving shade by leaving this codicil in his will: "For and in consideration of the great love I bear this tree and the great desire I have for its protection for all time, I convey possession of itself and the land within eight feet of it on all sides."

Hannah Smith reassures "The Tree That Owns Itself" that it's safe from those who'd turn it into wood chips and paper towels.

3

The words are inscribed on a marker at the base of the mighty oak. But, truth be told, the tree standing today within an enclosure of granite posts strung together by iron-link chain is not Colonel Jackson's exact-same *Quercus*. In 1942 high winds brought down the aging 100-foot-tall, 15-foot-around giant. To the rescue came the Athens Junior Ladies Garden Club, which grew a seedling from one of the deceased's acorns and planted it with appropriate pomp in 1946. From tiny acorns, as they say—today "Junior" is the strapping heir to his illustrious father's legacy.

The Tree That Owns Itself receives admirers daily in the Dearing Historic District, near downtown Athens. It's No. 38 on the tour map available at the Athens Welcome Center, 280 East Dougherty Street; (706) 353–1820 or (800) 653–0603; www.visitathensga.com.

Bound In Skin
Athens

A 400-year-old book in the Hargrett Rare Books Collection of the University of Georgia's Ilah Dunlap Little Memorial Library may be bound in human skin. That's right. A handwritten note inside Apollodurus, a small Greek and Latin book printed in 1599, attests: "This book is bound in human skin." But nobody knows for certain whether the tan leathery-looking binding is actually human epidermis or the hide of a different animal.

"An Athens family donated the book to the library," explains Chuck Barber, the library's head of manuscripts. "They apparently didn't know for certain, and unless a piece was chopped off and tested for DNA, there's no way of saying definitely one way or the other. People who hear about the book are usually disappointed when they see it—they're expecting to see fingerprints, tattoos, or some other marks. By the time the skin would be stretched and tanned, those marks would be erased,

THE LINGUA GEORGIA

Traveling around the state, you're naturally going to want to stop and talk with folks. But like any foreign country, you're sometimes going to hit a language barrier. Here are a few helpful hints to get you over the rough spots.

• When Georgians and other Southerners say they're "fixin'" to do something, it doesn't mean they're repairin' somethin'—they're studying on it or just working up steam to get around to it. For example: "I'm fixin' to carry sister down to the Winn-Dixie."

- "That dog won't hunt" isn't dissing a canine's intestinal fortitude; it's a polite way of saying "I question the veracity of your last statement."
- "Mash" is Southern for push, as in "I'm in a rush; would you mash the gas pedal just a little bit stouter?"
- "High as a Georgia pine" is a colorful way of saying "Mama's been in the cooking sherry again."
- "Lower than a snake's belly in a wheel rut" is code for "Bubber's a yellow dog, son-of-a-no-good skunk."
- "So good, you'll slap your granny" is a Ty Ty and Talking Rock way of saying "Emeril, eat your heart out."
- When someone in these parts puts on a big smile and declares, "Y'all come see us real soon, you heah," don't take it as an invitation to Sunday dinner. It's like saying "It's good seeing you." Maybe they think so, maybe they don't. And when they ask, "Howya doin'?" they don't really want to know.
- "Bless her heart": "Bless her heart, she's so bucktoothed she could eat corn on the cob through a picket fence."
- "Tar": "I run over a nail and got a flat tar."
- "Spire": What you keep in your trunk in case of a flat tar.
- "Fell off": "She's fell off so much, she don't hardly throw a shadow."
- "Delta is ready when you are": "I've heard how you do it up North one time too many."

anyway. If it is human skin, it's probably not some evil doing, where somebody was skinned alive to be turned into a book. Long ago, some people willed their skin to book lovers to perpetuate themselves after death." Now there's a really creepy thought.

The book is shown by request.

If you're here on Confederate Memorial Day, in late April, you can see one of the Old South's rarest documents: The original Constitution of the Confederate States of America is here at UGA, not in Richmond, as you might suppose. To find out more, contact the University of Georgia at (706) 542–0842; www.uga.edu.

Kissing Rocks
Athens

Oh, if this pile of boulders could talk, what tales it might tattle of young women kissing their beaus goodnight under the starry Georgia skies. A brass plaque on the mossy, tree-shaded rocks explains: "This area was a traditional meeting place during the period of 1892–1942 for the young ladies of the State Normal School and their beaus. From these meetings, the spot became known as 'The Kissing Rocks.'"

Attending a Normal School didn't imply anything about the students' position in the social strata. In the long ago that's what teachers' colleges were called. This one was folded into the University of Georgia's education department during World War II. When the U.S. Navy Supply Corps School took over the campus in the mid-1950s, that presumably was the end of the smooching around the old stones. Lovers who rendezvous on the rocks these days shouldn't be surprised if they have some apparitional onlookers. In the early 1950s University of Georgia archaeologists uncovered evidence of an ancient Indian campsite and burial grounds.

Although the U.S. Navy Supply Corps School, where the Kissing Rocks are situated, is scheduled to be whacked by the Pentagon's budget-cutting axe, the rocks will continue to inspire. They're on view every day at 1425 Prince Avenue, U.S. Highway 129.

Uga, "A Damn Good Dog"
Athens

For the past fifty-five years, Uga, a six-member line of English bulldogs raised by the Frank W. Seiler family of Savannah, has led the University of Georgia Bulldogs to Southeastern Conference football championships, postseason bowl victories, and a national championship. From Uga I (1956–66) through the reigning Uga VI, who assumed his duties in 1999, these "Damn Good Dogs," have appeared on the covers of national magazines and in movies, banquets, and parades. They've made appearances for the March of Dimes, Easter Seals, and other worthy causes.

Uga I was the grandson of a mascot that traveled with the team to the 1943 Rose Bowl. Uga II (1966–71) made his first appearance at Homecoming 1966, when the stadium throng thundered "Damn Good Dog," a chorus that has serenaded every Uga ever since. Uga III (1972–80) closed out his illustrious career by leading the biped Bulldogs to the NCAA national championship. His successor, Uga IV (1981–89), escorted Herschel Walker to New York for his 1982 Heisman Trophy acceptance. Uga V (1990–99) had a nonbarking role in the opening scene of *Midnight in the Garden of Good and Evil,* filmed in his hometown of Savannah. If Uga VI has his wish, he'll put a big bite on Florida's Gators, the Tennessee Vols, and Georgia Tech Yellow Jackets and lead his pals back to national glory.

Other school mascots may be forgotten when their time comes. When it's time for Uga to depart for the great kennel in the sky, he and his successors are the only collegiate mascots honored with burial in their home stadium. As 80,000 fans come through the main gate of Sanford Stadium for a UGA game, they place flowers and tributes on the vaults and Georgia marble epitaphs that hold the remains of their beloved canines. They pat the muzzle of his bronze likeness for good luck against the enemy and say, "Thank you, Uga," for taking over from that silly billy goat with a hat and ribboned horns that led Georgia onto the field for its first-ever game, against Auburn, in 1892.

The Uga Memorial is included in tours offered by the UGA Visitors Center, Four Towers Building, College Station Road; (706) 542–0842; www.uga.edu.

The ghosts of Ugas past welcome fans to Georgia Bulldog games at Athens's Sanford Stadium. Out on the field, the reigning Uga woofs it up as the Dawgs terrorize another opponent.

O, Little Town Of . . .

Bethlehem

Eleven months of the year, Bethlehem's two-room post office is as quiet as a church sanctuary on Thursday afternoon. But come December, the rectangular brown-brick building gets as busy as a pool room on payday. Hundreds of folks, many of them traveling a far piece to the one-stoplight Barrow County bump in the road, line up every day to have their Christmas mail postmarked with an image of the Magi and Christmas Greetings from Bethlehem.

People who live too far away to pilgrimage to Bethlehem send batches of cards to their friends in Georgia, who tote them over to the little town of. Most years the post office processes about 60,000 pieces of seasonal mail, but in the wake of the 9/11 tragedy, 2001 was a banner year. The prized postmark went on more than 150,000 holiday greetings.

"I think more people sent cards to keep in touch with family and friends," said Postmistress Cathy Montgomery. "With everything that's gone on, everybody seems to want to pull closer together. The holidays are a great time for doing that."

The Bethlehem Post Office is on Highway 11, a mile south of Highway 316/U.S. Highway 29 between Lawrenceville and Athens; (770) 867–6212.

WALKING THE A.T.: SHORT TAKES ON THE APPALACHIAN TRAIL

You, too, can walk the fabled Appalachian Trail, without risking blisters or scuffing your shiny new 10-league hiking boots. At Neel's Gap, U.S. Highway 19/129, between Dahlonega and Vogel State Park, the A.T. passes under a covered breezeway at the Mountain Crossings/Walasi-Yi Center (706–745–6095), the only place the 2,015-mile Georgia-to-Maine wilderness thruway goes indoors. After your exhausting few-feet hike, you can replenish your supplies, get trail information, have a hot shower, and share adventures with fellow hikers. If this exhilarating taste gets you craving for more, hitch up your backpack and huff and puff 5.7 moderately difficult miles to Tesnatee Gap on the Richard Russell Scenic Highway (Highway 348). If you're a novice at this outdoorsy stuff, have a bud waiting with a Bud, TLC, and Blistex.

The Goat and Peter the First
Buckhead

In the bucolic Morgan County community of Buckhead, the landscape is a pastoral palate of green fields, dairy cows, farmhouses, and silos. Behind the doors of a hulking stainless-steel warehouse, where you figure to behold John Deere tractors, hay balers, and such—wow! Walls are covered, salon style, with ceiling-to-floor oil paintings and watercolors of women in hats, nudes, Madonnas, European and American landscapes, mosaics, and sculptures of cats, goats, people, and saints. Welcome to the Steffen Thomas Museum and Archives. The namesake immigrated from Germany in the 1920s, settled in Atlanta, and, until his death in 1990 at age eighty-four, created a trove of Expressionist paintings, sculptures, and mosaics. His most celebrated works include the Alabama Memorial at the Vicksburg National Military Park in Mississippi and a bronze portrait bust of Dr. George Washington Carver at Alabama's Tuskegee University.

Among the "personal" pieces in the Morgan County museum is a welded-metal sculpture of the family's Siamese cat, Peter the First, a family icon with which children and grandchildren posed for photos. *The Goat of Mentelle* is the Expressionist self-portrait sculpture of the artist as a billy goat (he lived on Mentelle Street in Atlanta). The museum was created by Thomas's widow, Sara, who located the treasures on two acres adjoining a farm owned by the couple's son, Steffen Thomas Jr. The Steffen Thomas Museum and Archives is at 4200 Bethany Road, 3 miles off Interstate 20 at exit 121. Turn right and drive 2 miles to Bethany Road; turn right again; the museum is 1 mile down on the right. Open Tuesday through Saturday 11:00 A.M. to 4:00 P.M. Phone (706) 342–7557 or visit www.steffenthomas.org.

Come See Elvis Presley's . . . Wart?
Cornelia

Been to Graceland and think you've seen everything Elvis? Think again, Bubba. A toenail shard plucked from the Jungle Room's shag carpeting and a wart excised from the King's royal wrist are relics you'll see only in Joni Mabe's Panoramic Encyclopedia of Everything Elvis, on view at the Loudermilk Boarding House Museum in Cornelia.

"I've been collecting since the day he died on August 16, 1977," says self-described "Elvis Babe" and "Queen of the King" Mabe, who earned her master's in fine arts from the University of Georgia in 1983 with a thesis on her fallen idol. "I have over 30,000 items, and I'm still adding pieces. I've tried to show him as a real human being, I guess you could say warts and all, with faults like everybody else. I haven't heard of any larger private collection, and I'm sure mine's the most unique." She schlepped her tribute across the country and overseas for fourteen years; in 2000 she laid her precious burden down in her great-grandparents' 1908 Victorian boardinghouse.

Hundreds of photos capture Elvis svelte and porky, alive and wiggling on stage, and "sighted" from Mobile to Monte Carlo years after death. He's banner headlines in scores of newspaper and magazine articles ("Nixon Was Grooming Elvis for President," the *National Examiner* declares. "If it hadn't been for his untimely death, the King of Rock and Roll might be sitting in the Oval Office today").

No Elvis shrine anywhere, not even Graceland, has a keepsake more personal than the "Elvis Wart" in Joni Mabe's Panoramic Encyclopedia of Everything Elvis. "Elvis Babe" and "Queen of the King" Mabe acquired the dermatological detritus from the doctor who excised it before Presley enlisted in the army. Doubters can check it out in a presurgery photo.

His image is pasted on pelvis-shaking Elvis dolls and clocks, key rings, plates, playing cards, trading cards, mugs, scarves, towels, "I Just Wanna Be Your Teddy Bear"(s), T-shirts, cartoons, and books (*On the Throne with the King: the Ultimate Elvis Bathroom Trivia Book*). Mabe even paid $5.00 for a vial of "Elvis Sweat" at a New York novelty store.

"Everything in the collection is special," Mabe declares, "but the wart and toenail are the most priceless. I found the toenail in the shag carpet in the Jungle Room at Graceland, and I bought the wart from his doctor, who removed it before Elvis went into the service."

Displayed in a glass case, the nail shard, with a photo of the Jungle Room, is labeled "the Maybe Elvis Toenail" because, barring DNA testing, not even "The Queen of the King" can be swear-on-a-stack-of-Bibles certain it's his and not some feckless fan's detritus. She harbors no doubts whatever that a wrist wart clearly visible in a photo of Elvis is the same grisly gray nodule preserved in a medical vial. (Mabe's e-mail, by the way, is elviswart@Jonimabe.com.) The gift shop stocks Elvis books, posters, mugs, T-shirts, scarves, and Mabe's own kingly artwork.

"The Big E Celebration," honoring his August death anniversary, is the Loudermilk Museum's biggest day. Elvis impersonators moan "Love Me Tender" and "Don't Be Cruel" and wrap sweaty scarves around admirers' necks. They toast his memory with the King's fave peanut butter and banana sandwiches and MoonPies (lunar-shaped cake-and-marshmallow confections, traditionally paired with RC Cola, like champagne and caviar that delighted the royal sweet tooth.)

Somewhere in the great somewhere, a candle glows. The honored guest gives the royal wave and tips his crown. "Thankya, Joni, thankya-verymuch."

The Loudermilk Boarding House Museum is at 271 Foreacre Street, Cornelia; (706) 778–2001; www.jonimabe.com. It's 80 miles northeast of Atlanta on Interstate 85/985. Take a self-guided tour Friday and Saturday 10:00 A.M. to 5:00 P.M. Admission fee.

The Big Red Apple
Cornelia

Elvis was still a far-off gleam in Vernon and Gladys Presley's eyes when Cornelia planted its Big Red Apple. English and Canadian growers introduced Habersham County to Red Delicious, Stayman, Winesap, Granny Smith, and other juicy fruit in the early 1900s. By 1926 apples were so much the apple of Habersham's eye that a monument was deemed a fitting tribute. With visions of fried pies and apple butter dancing in their heads, bands, puffed-up politicians, hundreds of townsfolk, and Apple Blossom Queen Catherine Neal turned out in front of the train depot for Le Grande Pomme's coming out. All these years, the 5,200-pound apple—7 feet tall, 22 feet around—has pirouetted on its pedestal, defying winds, worms, and school-boy vandals. Alas, the old depot hasn't heard a train whistle since we liked Ike and loved Lucy.

How many fried pies could a homemaker make from the 5,200-pound Big Red Apple in Cornelia? If it wasn't made out of cement, they could probably whip up about a kazillion. English and Canadian growers introduced Granny Smith, Red Delicious, and their kin to the green hills of Habersham County nearly a century ago.

CORNELIA

HOME OF THE BIG RED APPLE

HABERSHAM COUNTY GEORGIA

RC COLA AND MOONPIE

"RC Cola and MoonPie" go together like Mason and Dixon and PB&J. It's a Southern thing that's been going on since 1917, when the Chattanooga Bakery in Chattanooga, Nearly-in-Georgia, Tennessee, began producing the tasty little chocolate-frosted cake with the marshmallow filling. How Moon-Pie ("The Only One on the Planet") got linked in the Southern psyche with RC (Royal Crown) Cola, founded in Columbus, Georgia, in 1905, is one of life's imponderables. The two products have no corporate links and have never done joint promotions. One theory is that Southern working people paired them during the Great Depression because the luxury of a MoonPie and a twelve-ounce RC required only a thin-dime investment.

Historians credit Chattanooga Bakery traveling supplier Earl Mitchell Sr. with inventing the MoonPie. The story goes that while Mitchell was working his territory in the Kentucky and West Virginia coal fields in the early 1900s, he asked miners in a company store what they might like as a snack. The miners ruminated on it awhile and reckoned such a snack had to fit in their lunch pails and be solid, filling, and not necessarily good for them. "About how big should it be?" Mitchell wanted to know. A miner looked out the store's screen door and framed the full moon with his large hands. "That big," he declared.

When Mitchell got back to the bakery, he asked company "engineers" to create the coal miner's lunar vision. They came up with a pair of graham cookies, sandwiching a marshmallow filling, and coated with chocolate frosting. It was an overnight sensation. By the 1950s the bakery was working so hard to keep up with the MoonPie demand that it discontinued all its other products. About 300,000 come off the assembly lines every day, some destined for shipment to snackers as far away as Japan, where they're known as Massai Pie. MPs also come with vanilla and butterscotch frosting, but purists insist on the old faithful original.

Columbus can't claim the birthplace of Coca-Cola (see Southwest chapter), but RC's roots are indisputably deep in the Chattahoochee River city. In the early 1900s Claud A. Hatcher, a graduate pharmacist, began creating his own soft drinks in the basement of his family's wholesale grocery business. One of his "experiments" evolved into RC, the flagship of America's third-largest soft drink company. The "family" now includes the Nehi line of fruit-flavored drinks.

Nobody's quite sure why, but RC Cola and MoonPie have gone together like love and marriage, a horse and carriage, since the early 1900s. RC was formulated in Columbus, and MoonPies in Chattanooga-Nearly-in-Georgia, Tennessee.

The Yellow Hills of Georgia
Dahlonega

California had a nice little spell of gold fever in 1849, but two decades before Sutter's Mill got everybody hopping, the first bona fide gold rush in the USA took place in the northeast Georgia hills around Dahlonega. Local lore has it that a trapper named Benjamin Parks stubbed his toe on a rock in a mountain stream; when the rock winked bright yellow, he forgot his abused toe and shouted the north Georgia rendition of "Eureka, I have found it!" and sent fortune hunters scrambling into the rugged country 60 miles north of the future metropolis of Atlanta. Some struck it rich. Those whom fortune shunned moved on to California after much richer mother lodes were discovered there.

Dahlonega, which sprang up around the mines, is a distortion of the Cherokee word for "yellow." Between 1829 and 1839, the hills around here gave up $20 million in gold. Much of it was hauled over to the town's branch of the U.S. Mint, which from 1838 to 1861, when the Civil War shut it down, turned out $6 million in coins. Although mining is no longer a big industry, tourists—who *are* a big industry—pan for glittery pebbles in a sluice at Crisson's Mine (706–864–6363) and take a guided forty-five-minute walk through the shafts of the Consolidated Mine, which closed in 1906. Enough gold is scraped up to periodically regild the Georgia Capitol dome in Atlanta and the spire of North Georgia College's administration building, on the site of the former U.S. Mint, down the way from the Dahlonega town square.

The Dahlonega Gold Museum State Historic Site, in the 1836 Greek Revival courthouse on the town square, tells the story of the gold rush and the many mines that once flourished here. Secured in alarmed cases on the main floor are Dahlonega-minted coins and nuggets, including a whopper weighing close to six ounces. Old-timers whose families worked in the mines in the late nineteenth and early twentieth centuries tell their tales in a twenty-eight-minute documentary film upstairs in the old courtroom.

Those thrilling days of yesteryear are relived during Gold Rush Days the third weekend of October. The Gold Museum is open daily. Admission fee. Call (706) 864–6962 or (800) 864–PARK or visit www.gastateparks .org. From Atlanta take Highway 400 north to Highway 60; turn left and drive 5 miles to Dahlonega's town square.

There's still enough gold in them thar hills around Dahlonega to intrigue tourists who pan for flecks and flakes at sluices in the town where America's first bona fide gold rush took place in the 1820s.

Georgia's Stonehenge
Elbert County

We don't have to travel to England's Salisbury Plain to see Stonehenge. We have our own, right here in Elbert County. Like the 4,000-year-old original, the 19-foot-tall Georgia Guidestones are six rectangular granite slabs aligned astronomically. The central stone is surrounded by four similar stones radiating from the center like spokes on a wagon wheel. A smaller sixth stone across the top caps the monument. Peeking through a narrow slit running through the central slab, it's possible to site the summer and winter solstices and fall and spring equinoxes through the stones. Idealistic maxims in English, Russian, Hebrew, Arabic, Hindi, Spanish, Chinese, Sanskrit, and Swahili carved into the stones in 4-inch-high characters read:

- BE NOT A CANCER ON THE EARTH, LEAVE ROOM FOR NATURE.

- PRIZE TRUTH, BEAUTY, LOVE, SEEKING HARMONY WITH THE FINITE.

- LET ALL NATIONS RULE INTERNALLY RESOLVING EXTERNAL DISPUTES IN A WORLD COURT.

- AVOID PETTY LAWS AND USELESS OFFICIALS.

- UNITE HUMANITY WITH A LIVING NEW LANGUAGE.

- GUIDE REPRODUCTION WISELY, IMPROVING FITNESS AND DIVERSITY.

- RULE PASSION, FAITH, TRADITION AND ALL THINGS WITH TEMPERED REASON.

- PROTECT PEOPLE AND NATIONS WITH FAIR LAWS AND JUST COURTS.

The origin of the Guidestones is as mysterious as the stones themselves. In 1979 a man with the admitted pseudonym "Robert C. Christian" established an escrow account with an Elberton bank to finance the monument. The banker who handled the transaction reportedly carried the secret to his grave, but "Mr. Christian's" vision stands in a field on Highway 77, 7.2 miles north of Elberton.

Is it Stonehenge on England's Salisbury Plain? Nope, it's the Georgia Guidestones on a pasture in rural Elbert County.

"Dutchy"
Elberton

Elbert County's renown as "Granite Capital of the World," with forty-five quarries and 150 finishing companies, began on an unpromising note. In 1898 sculptor Arthur Beter was commissioned to create a memorial to the county's Confederate dead. The first monument ever made from the county's abundant bluish-gray stone, it would stand tall and defiant on a pedestal in Elberton's town square. When the 7-foot soldier was unveiled, Rebel yells turned to jeers and stunned silence. The figure's tunic-style uniform and cap looked suspiciously like those worn by the Union Army, and Beter's loyalty to the lost Confederate cause was questioned. Fearing for his safety, the sculptor fled and never returned.

When a wisecracker suggested that the stony-faced soldier resembled a hybrid of a hippopotamus and a Pennsylvania Dutchman, the statue was derisively dubbed "Dutchy." On August 16, 1900, the statue was pulled down from its pedestal with a lynching noose twisted around his neck and broke into three pieces. Two days later he was buried facedown at the base of the pedestal, an "honor" usually reserved for executed traitors. Poor Dutchy lay moldering in his grave until April 1982, when the Elberton Granite Association exhumed his remains, ran him through a car wash, and put him back together in the Elberton Granite Museum & Exhibit, where he stands today in a place of honor. The twist to the story is that from Dutchy's tortured seed has sprung Elbert County's multimillion-dollar granite industry. Most of it goes into grave stones, but parts of the U.S. Capitol and other monuments, post offices, and public buildings coast to coast were made in Elbert County.

The Elberton Granite Museum & Exhibit is at 1 Granite Plaza, off Highway 17/72 in Elberton; (706) 283–2551; www.egaonline.com. The museum is open Monday through Saturday 2:00 to 5:00 P.M.

Alas, poor Dutchy,
we hardly knew ye.
Damned, lynched,
buried, resurrected, and
redeemed, he now lies in state
in the Elberton Granite Museum.

"Old Dan Tucker"
Elberton

Old Dan Tucker, he got drunk,
He fell in the fire, and kicked up a chunk,
A coal of fire got in his shoe,
And, oh, my Lord, how the ashes flew.
Old Dan Tucker was a grand old man,
He washed his face in a frying pan,
He combed his hair with a wagon wheel,
And he died with a toothpick in his heel.

Like many a folk tune passed down through the generations, the one about Old Dan Tucker was based on a real-life, flesh-and-blood nonfiction character. During the late 1700s, the Reverend Daniel Tucker operated a ferry on the Savannah River in today's Elbert County. He ministered to slaves, who immortalized him in a tune that kept growing verses long after he was buried in the Tucker Cemetery, which sits on Heardmont Road, on a bluff overlooking the Savannah River's Richard B. Russell Lake. If you'd like to pay your respects, get directions from the Elbert County Welcome Center; (706) 283–5651 or (800) 992–1039; www.elbertga.com.

A Little Pink in the Middle, Please
Flowery Branch

In the early 1900s Rachel and Rilla Porter did the cooking at their family's restaurant at Flowery Branch, a railroad whistle-stop near Gainesville. Traveling salesmen, trainmen, and rail riders raved so much about the Porter's way with beef that word spread up and down the land. Pretty soon, "Porterhouse steak" was on menus coast to coast. A New York saloon also claims the honor—but don't you believe it.

ROBERT TOOMBS AND "LITTLE ALEX"

Confederate Secretary of State Robert Toombs and Vice President Alexander Hamilton Stephens lived within a horseback ride of each other in Washington and Crawfordville, respectively. The tall, stocky Toombs and frail, invalid "Little Alex," as he was called, were good friends who often found themselves on the opposite side of issues. On one occasion the two passed outside a courthouse in Greensboro, where they were to debate. Toombs pointed to Stephens and shouted: "Look at that little fellow. If you'd grease him up and pin his ears back, you could swallow him whole." Undaunted, the feisty Stephens shot back: "Yes, and you'd have more brains in your stomach than you have in your head." The statesmen are remembered at the Robert Toombs State Historic Site in Washington and A. H. Stephens State Park in Crawfordville. For information about both, call (800) 864–PARK, or visit www.gastate parks.org.

Redeeming General Longstreet
Gainesville

Southerners licking their wounds after Appomattox needed somebody to blame. They couldn't rebuke sainted Bobby Lee, so they hit on "Lee's Old Warrior." Lieutenant General James Longstreet was an easy target. As Lee's second in command at Gettysburg, he had argued in vain with the great one over tactics and been proven right. So, illogically, the Confederacy's Waterloo must have been Longstreet's doing. To boot, he was a prewar abolitionist and a postwar Republican, a friend of Ulysses S. Grant, a Catholic in the Bible Belt, commander of the all-black Louisiana National Guard, and an outspoken advocate of the South's peaceful acceptance of the war's outcome. Forced out of New Orleans in 1875, he returned to his native northeast Georgia—where he was accepted, if not warmly embraced—and spent his last twenty-nine years.

Old wartime comrades checked into the Piedmont Hotel in Gainesville, which he ran until the early 1890s. Future President Woodrow Wilson's daughter, Jesse, was even born in the hotel in 1887. When Longstreet died in 1904, at age eighty-three, 3,000 Confederate veterans saw him to his rest in Gainesville's Alta Vista Cemetery. The old Piedmont Hotel was reportedly razed in 1918, but in 1996 historians made a startling discovery—the lower level of its three-story north wing, including Woodrow Wilson's old rooms, had escaped demolition and was doing business as a rooming house. The Longstreet Society, founded in 1994, purchased the building with plans to convert it to a visitor center and museum that will chronicle Longstreet's boyhood on a Georgia farm, his service as an Indian fighter on the western frontier, a hero of the 1840s Mexican War, a U.S. army major at the start of the Civil War, and postwar peacemaker, U.S. Postmaster, President Grant's minister to Turkey, commissioner of U.S. railroads, author, inventor, and patriot. With the passage of time and generations—and movies such as the made-for-TV *Gettysburg* and the novel *Killer Angels*—old animosities have evaporated like the Dixie dew. In 2001 the United Daughters of the Confederacy dedicated a standing, life-size statue of Longstreet at the site of his former Gainesville farm. Elsewhere in town, a Baptist church, pediatric and OB–GYN clinics, and a mortgage company are named for him. A giant Stars and Stripes flutters over his grave in Alta Vista Cemetery, 521 Jones Street; (770) 535–6883. Contact the Longstreet Society at (770) 539–9005.

Once a pariah to diehard advocates of the lost Confederate cause, who blamed him for Bobby Lee's blunders at Gettysburg, Lieutenant General James Longstreet now rests in peace in Gainesville's Alta Vista Cemetery. A giant Stars and Stripes flies above him, and a small Confederate Stars and Bars is stuck in the ground next to his gravestone.

The Big Rooster
Gainesville

"Isn't that just like a man?" a Gainesville woman fumes. "Women do all the work and a man takes the credit." Her beef: Hens lay the eggs that assure the continuity of the poultry industry that's saluted by the Poultry Monument in downtown Gainesville's Poultry Park. But who do you think stands atop the granite shaft? Not a lady hen, no sirree, but a bronze rooster brazenly preening his tail feathers. The noble hen and a cache of eggs get the bottom of the shaft.

A plaque hails Gainesville as "the cradle of the poultry industry, inseparately linked since World War II, when pioneering efforts by the industry's greatest names transformed the 'barnyard hen' into the First Lady of industrial agriculture and turned the eyes of the world toward Gainesville as the cradle and capital of the modern poultry industry. The nucleus of this agricultural explosion was located a hundred feet east of this spot, where in the wake of Gainesville's catastrophic 1936 tornado, one poultryman began putting together all aspects of the poultry production cycle into a vertically integrated operation that did for the poultry industry what Henry Ford did for automobile manufacturing."

Another plaque hails poultry's exemplary nutritional value and asks: "What would our holiday traditions be like without turkey, the staple of the first settlers and Benjamin Franklin's choice as our national emblem?"

Poultry Park is in downtown Gainesville (Interstate 985, exit 22) at West Academy Street and Jesse Jewell Parkway, a main thoroughfare named for Gainesville's Henry Ford of the poultry bidness. For more, contact the Gainesville-Hall County Convention & Visitors Bureau, 117 Jesse Jewell Parkway; Gainesville; (770) 536–5209 or (888) 536–0005; www.gainesvillehallcvb.org.

Say It Ain't So, Old Joe
Gainesville

Is Gainesville's Johnny Reb—gasp!—really a Yankee in disguise?

Proudly commanding the city's downtown square, the 28-foot-tall statue of the Confederate soldier known as "Old Joe" looks sternly northward, clutching a rifle atop a marble column festooned with the Rebel battle flag.

Old Joe's belt buckle is engraved with the initials "CSA," for Confederate States of America. A plaque declares his dedication to "Southern Convictions." But beneath Joe's bronze casting is a long-held secret, betrayed by his kit bag with the letters "U.S." His weapon is the biggest giveaway. It's a model of a Springfield rifle dating from 1873, eight years after Appomattox.

Old Joe's Yankee heritage can be traced back to a shortage of Yankee dollars. The post–Civil War South didn't have a lot, so in 1898, when the Gainesville chapter of the United Daughters of the Confederacy could only raise $2,500, they had to settle for a "Rebbed-up" version of a Spanish-American War soldier.

Far from being edified by the discovery, Gainesville's most ardent Civil War buffs are downright livid. Athens architect Garland Reynolds, who revealed Old Joe's true identity, says he was "almost run out of town" by a few of the most incensed diehards.

Longstreet's Feisty Widow
Gainesville

Helen Dortch Longstreet, widow of Confederate Lieutenant General James Longstreet, inherited her famous husband's appetite for hopeless causes. The thirty-four-year-old Helen Dortch married the seventy-five-year-old former general in 1897. Asked why she married a man old enough to be her grandfather, she replied, "Because I love him, for no woman would marry a man she did not love. When he asked for my hand, I granted it, knowing I was entrusting my life and happiness to one of the noblest men God ever created."

After his death in 1904, she struck out on her own as an author, editor, lecturer, civic leader, and political and social pot-boiler. She was lauded for her work with the troops during the Spanish-American War and World War I. She was Georgia's first female postmaster and worked as "Helen the Riveter" at a World War II B-29 bomber plant. Her book, *Lee and Longstreet at High Tide,* defended her husband's actions at the Battle of Gettysburg.

Before women had the right to vote, she had the starch to take on the icons of Georgia politics and industry. In 1912, she went to war with the Georgia Power Company over the utility conglomerate's plans to harness Tallulah Falls in northeast Georgia's spectacular Tallulah Gorge for a hydroelectric dam. She wanted to preserve the gorge as a state park, but lost in the all-male legislature and the courts. She also lost her mortgaged home when owners of resort hotels and other tourist businesses reneged on promises to help her with court costs. The sixty-three-acre lake created by the 116-foot-high dam swallowed the cataracts once known as "The Niagara of the South."

In 1995, the Longstreet Society's proposal to put her name on an interpretive center at the new Tallulah Gorge State Park was vetoed by the Georgia Department of Natural Resources, which developed the park in partnership with Georgia Power (big utilities have long memories). The Jane Hurt Yarn Interpretive Center was named, instead, for "Georgia's Grand Lady of Conservation" (1924–1995). Mrs. L got second prize: The Helen Dortch Longstreet Trail System around the gorge and lake created by the dam recognizes her as "one of Georgia's first conservationists, who worked tirelessly to protect Tallulah Gorge."

Well into her eighties, Mrs. Longstreet mounted a 1940s write-in campaign for governor against Herman Talmadge, scion of one of the state's most famous political clans. Her quixotic windmill tilt didn't make a dent in cigar-chompin' "Hummon." She got barely one hundred votes statewide. Talmadge served many years as governor and U.S. Senator and died in 2002. Mrs. Longstreet was a year short of a century when she went to join her general in 1962.

The Iron Horse

Greene County

In 1954 sculptor Abbot Pattison placed a 2,000-pound horse, fashioned from scrap iron, on the University of Georgia campus in Athens. Did the students appreciate Pattison's gift horse? Why, no; the heathens took a hint from Homer and attacked it with hacksaws and other weapons of mass destruction. To keep the beleaguered steed from reverting to scrap, two days after its Athens debut, a UGA professor trucked it off to his Greene County farm. There it safely grazes behind a fence in a field off Highway 15 at the Oconee River Bridge.

The Old Gaol

Greensboro

If Greene Countians ever decided to reenact the French Revolution, they could start by sacking the Greensboro "gaol." Whether or not it really was modeled after the Parisian Bastille, as some declare, the fortress is one scary-looking place. Completed in 1807, its grim granite walls, 2 feet thick with small barred windows and a crenellated roofline, were intended to warn citizens to stay on the straight and narrow. Those who faltered were imprisoned in medieval dungeons wet, dark, and cold. Those paying the ultimate price for their sins were dropped, with a noose around their necks, through a second-floor trapdoor. With no civil libertarians to adjudicate for comfier facilities, poor wretches moldered in the gloomy garrison until 1895. The Old Gaol is on East Greene Street, behind the courthouse. If you'd like to serve a brief sentence, call (706) 453–7592 for an appointment.

A BRIDGE NOT TOO FAR

Watson Mill Covered Bridge, a spectacular 229-foot span, gets undisputed honors as the state's longest covered bridge. Stovall Mill Bridge, on Highway 225 North between Helen and Batesville, takes the prize as the smallest covered bridge you can visit. Built in 1895 by sawmill, gristmill, and shingle mill operator Fred Stovall, the picturesque queen post-style pedestrian span over Chickamauga Creek measures 36.8 feet from portal to portal. Spread lunch on the picnic table while you admire the mountain greenery and the bridge's classical lines. Movie buffs of a certain age might remember adopted Georgian Susan Hayward trodding Stovall's planks in the 1951 movie *I'd Climb the Highest Mountain*, a vintage weepy about the rough-as-a-cob life of a mountain minister and his wife, who endured all without breaking a nail or mussing a hair. Six years after she made that movie, Miss Hayward married a Georgia man and moved to Carrollton, where she's buried beside him in a Catholic church cemetery.

The Center of the World
Hart County

At a time, way back when many Europeans thought the earth was flat, Cherokees in north Georgia knew it was round and had a center. It was "Ah-Yek-A-Li-A-Lo-Hee," a Cherokee phrase for Center of the World. On a plateau, near the headwaters of four creeks, at the junction of numerous trails radiating in all directions, "Ah-Yek" was the site of tribal councils and trade among themselves and with early white settlers.

Unfortunately, the Cherokees were uprooted from the center of their world by the tragic Trail of Tears that sent them forcibly west of the Mississippi in the 1830s. In a too-little-too-late effort to make amends, the Daughters of the American Revolution (DAR) put up a large Elberton granite monument at the site in 1923. A marker erected by the Georgia Historical Commission in 1954 reads: " This was Al-Yek-lions-lo-Hee [it has various spellings], the Center of the World to the Cherokee Indians. To this assembly ground, from which trails radiate in many directions, they came to hold their Councils, to dance and worship, which to them were related functions."

The Center of the World is on U.S. Highway 29, four miles southwest of Hartwell. For information contact the Hart County Chamber of Commerce, 83 Depot Street, Hartwell; (706) 376–8590; www .hart-chamber.org.

Bavaria Meets the Blue Ridge
Helen

Once upon the early 1900s there was a little mountain hamlet called Helen. It was named for the favorite daughter of the owner of a big logging company, because, in truth, the town earned its daily succor from brawny men who cut the trees that covered the mountainsides and hauled them to Helen's sawmills. When all the cuttable trees were cut and the loggers no longer logged and the sawmills no longer sawed, alas, poor Helen was abandoned like a red-headed stepchild. But hark! In the 1960s a bright young fellow—who sounded a lot like Mickey Rooney in *Love Finds Andy Hardy*—said to the remaining townsfolk: "Hey, kids, let's put on a show!" This bright young fellow had traveled in Germany, and had been charmed by fairy-tale castles, cuckoo clocks, and geranium boxes wherever he turned. So the "show" he had in mind would be a full-scale, never-ending Bavarian stage set. The people said, okeydokey, for it was either be Bavarian or be a chicken plucker down in Gainesville.

They went to work, and, before you knew it, "Alpine Helen" was born. Every old building in town—and new ones with Europey-looking arcades and twisty little lanes and balconies—got a red-tile roof, geranium boxes, and stucco walls with murals of contented dairy cows and edelweiss. Cuckoo clocks chirped and chimed wherever you turned an ear. To give flatlanders

Why fly all the way to Europe, when you can clip-clop though "Alpine Helen" in a horse-drawn fiaker like those in Vienna and Munich? While you're cruising through town, set your sights on shop windows laden with leder-hosen, Limburger, cuckoo clocks, and Tyrolean hats.

motivation for the trip, enterprising folks opened beer gardens, where you can tilt back Lowenbrau and knock off a plate of bratwurst and wienerschnitzel, while accordionists wheeze out schmaltzy waltzes and big hits from *The Sound of Music*. Shops put out year-round Christmas frippery, lederhosen, dirndls, Tyrolean hats, chocolate truffles, strudel and Black Forest cake, "stinky socks" cheeses, good deals at Gap and Banana Republic outlets, and great stuff imported from Germany, Switzerland, Norway, Mexico, Costa Rica, and Taiwan—and a cuckoo clock for every household.

Four decades after the red-headed stepchild turned into a Bavarian grand duchess, purists scorn it—some, I'm sorry to say, cruelly lambaste it—but every year three million persons vote with their feet, shout "Jawohl, Helen," and cheerfully unload their wallets. The biggest waves come for the fall Oktoberfest, when the hills are alive with the sounds of "oom-pah-pah" and the Chicken Dance. In warm weather they scoot through town on inner tubes over the mild rapids of the Chattahoochee River, which comes out of the ground a few miles up in the hills. Throughout the year they clop through town in horse-drawn buggies, like the fiakers in Munich and Vienna; tour a mountains museum, a model railroad exhibit, and a bear and reptile park; go for horseback and hot air balloon rides; pan for gold; sample Georgia wines; play Alpine miniature golf; visit the Alpine Amusement Park; buy spirits at the Alpine Package Store; see the Alpine Auto and Buggy Museum; and get hitched at the Alpine Wedding Chapel. When visitors have exhausted all that, the Georgia Alps are just a yodel away.

To prepare yourselves for "gemutlichkeit," Georgia mountains style, get advance reconnaissance from the Alpine Helen–White County Convention & Visitors Bureau; (706) 878–2181 or (800) 858–8027; www.helenga.org. When you arrive, stop by the office at 726 Brucken Strasse. They've got a line on the best deals on lederhosen and cuckoo clocks.

THE BRIDGES OF NORTHEAST GEORGIA

Once upon the nineteenth century, more than 200 covered bridges carried walkers, horseback riders, buggies, wagons, and carriages over Georgia's rivers and streams. Most have fallen down, been torn down in the name of "progress," or been chopped into firewood. Two of the most picturesque survivors are 20-something miles apart east and west of Athens. The 229-foot-long Watson Mill Covered Bridge is the state's longest original-site covered bridge. Built over the South Fork River in 1885, it was named for Gabriel Watson, who built a gristmill there. Nowadays, the majestic town lattice truss–style bridge is the centerpiece of Watson Mill Bridge State Park, a 1,018-acre haven with camping, canoeing, fishing, picnic grounds, and biking and hiking trails. On sultry summer afternoons, cool off with a splash in the river's shoals under the bridge. The park is off Highway 22, 3 miles south of Comer. Call (706) 783–5349.

William McKinley was president when Elder Covered Bridge carried the first carriages over Rose Creek in 1897. In the early 1920s the venerable bridge was taken apart and moved to its present home on Highway 15, 4 miles south of Watkinsville. It's one of the state's last bridges of any type that still carries traffic without support from underlying steel beams. After visiting the dozens of artists' studios and galleries around Watkinsville and Oconee County, stop by the old bridge for a pastoral picnic and show-and-tell.

It looks a little lopsided, but not to worry. The Elder Covered Bridge has safely carried traffic since the 1920s, when it was moved to Highway 15, 4 miles south of Watkinsville. If you're afoot, you might want to be alert for wasps and other territorial stingers that nest in the rafters.

"Take a Deep Breath and Count to Ten . . ."
Jefferson

James M. Venable, a gentleman of Jefferson, was the first man on earth to hear those words from a physician. On March 30, 1842, Dr. Crawford Williamson Long, a twenty-six-year-old country doctor, laid an ether-soaked handkerchief over Venable's face. Before he could get halfway to ten, Venable crashed into unconsciousness, and Long removed tumors from his neck. Venable awakened with no memory of his ordeal, which should have gone down in medical history as the first painless surgery with anesthesia. Alas, alack, by the time Dr. Long published his discovery, others had also found the secret. But don't tell that to people in tiny Jefferson, where Dr. Long is still No. 1.

The Crawford W. Long Museum has a detailed diorama depicting James Venable's historic surgery. One of the most astonishing artifacts is his bill, an aspirin-sized $2.50. The museum is in a Greek Revival building at 28 College Street in downtown Jefferson; (706) 367–5307; www.crawford long.org. The museum is open Tuesday through Saturday. Admission fee. Take I–85 exit 137/US 129, and go south 6 miles to Jefferson.

By the grace of General Billy T. Sherman, "the best small town in America" was spared the fires of the Civil War. Now fair Madison is bracing for invasion by sprawling Atlanta.

"The Best Small Town in America"

Madison

What's the best small town in the whole U.S. of A.? In July 2000 *Travel Holiday* magazine answered: Why, Madison, Georgia, where else? The editors cited the town of 5,000's low crime rate, pretty good schools, cultural options, and civilized pace of life as points that won the prize over hundreds of other towns coast to coast. But all it really took to capture the jaded journalists' hearts was a walk through the spellbinding beauty of Madison's downtown historic district, where tree-shaded streets with a golden horde of antebellum and Victorian homes channel into a picture-perfect town square ringed by antiques shops, art galleries, an old-timey drug store, cafes with sidewalk tables, and a majestic early-twentieth-century courthouse. "It's the rare kind of town," the editors sighed, "where pulling up a rocking chair on a big shady front porch, mint julep in hand, still counts as a day well spent." Pish-posh if Madisonians have to drive 30 miles to Athens for a movie, a shopping mall, or a traffic jam entangling more than three vehicles.

Madison was here for the editors to gush over and pin a ribbon on because in 1864 General Sherman couldn't find it in his flinty heart to torch it. Late in 1864, with Atlanta a pile of ashes 60 miles to the west, Sherman and his Union firebrands marched up to Madison's doorstep with torches in hand and mischief on their minds. There to meet them was former U.S. Senator Joshua Hill, a secession opponent who'd met Sherman before the war. Hill surrendered the town, and Sherman told his disappointed troops: "Boys, this town's too doggone purty to burn, so what say we don't and say we did. There's bound to be some places down the road, like Atlanta back there, that could use a good burning." So they marched in and out again, with matches scorching a figurative hole in their pockets, and took out their frustrations on the rest of the state.

Today, invaders dropping by the visitor center on the square are handed matchbooks with the slogan THE TOWN SHERMAN REFUSED TO BURN. Townsfolk hope their guests have a wonderful time, leave stacks of green in antiques and folk arts shops, and put away a fine supper with a bottle of wine, before, like Sherman, they march out of town.

The more things change, the more they remain the same. In the 1860s Madisonians cried, "The Yankees are comin'! The Yankees are comin'!" Nowadays, they're crying, "Atlanta's comin'! Atlanta's comin'!" Sure enough, the metropolis is marching eastward, sweeping farmlands and sweet country towns under its skirts, threatening to bulldoze Madison's Norman Rockwell lifestyle into a chaos of subdivisions, fast food strips, and traffic. "Calling Senator Hill! Senator Hill to the barricades!" Check it out at the Madison–Morgan County Convention & Visitors Bureau, 115 East Jefferson Street; (706) 709–7406; www.madisonga .com. Madison is at I–20 exit 114/U.S. Highway 441, 60 miles east of Atlanta.

Which Came First, the Chicken or the Wabbit?

Rabbittown

During the Great Depression, when raising chickens was still a backyard nonindustry, Hall Countians earned their daily manna from bunny rabbits, which weren't bred for twitchy-nose cuteness but for sustenance that helped Gainesville and Hall County through hardscrabble times. With the post–World War II ascendency of chickens, Bugs and friends may now safely graze. But in honor of cottontail's noble sacrifice, the community on Gainesville's north side where they gave their all was named Rabbittown. In 1993 the "Hoppin' Little Place" chipped in for a very big stone "wabbit" (as Elmer Fudd would say).

What's up, Doc? For one thing, the Big Rabbit is way up on a stone pedestal in Rabbittown, "A Hoppin' Little Place" on the periphery of Gainesville. Br'er (or Sis) Rabbit is a tribute to the industry that prevailed here long before shrewder heads thought of turning chickens into big business. You can get anything you want, except rabbit, at the Rabbittown Cafe.

Br'er/Sis Rabbit waves a hospitable, 20-foot "howdy" in front of the Rabbittown Cafe (2415 Old Cornelia Highway, I–985 exit 24; 770–287–3695; www.rabbittowncafe.com). They're open daily including Sunday, when every church in the county seems to empty into the dining room. The cafeteria line dishes up grits; "cathead" biscuits and pork sausage; fried chicken, catfish, and BBQ; okra, collards, and candied yams; banana pudding and other fruits of the Southern table. Fajitas and other Tex-Mex dishes are a curtsy to the Hispanic community that is the backbone of Hall County's poultry business. The homey dining room is decorated with folksy drawings and soft-sculpture and ceramic bunnies, but the menu's completely hareless.

The Rabbittown Celebration, Saturday a week before Easter, brings families and friends together for breakfast at the cafe, followed by an Easter parade, Easter egg hunt, gospel singing, and clog dancing. Need a disposable camera to immortalize the festivities? Hop across the road to the Kangaroo Food Mart.

Ellicott Rock Wilderness
Rabun County

Northeast Georgia shares with North Carolina and South Carolina a three-quarter Deep South equivalent of the Southwest's Four Corners Junction. The remote sector of the Chattahoochee, Oconee, and Sumter National Forests was the focus of a 1960s boundary spat between Georgia and South Carolina, which, happily, was resolved without a rerun of Fort Sumter. To keep the peace, the Ellicott Rock Wilderness became part of the National Wilderness System in 1975, safeguarded by the

1964 National Wilderness Protection Act. Don't come to "Three Corners" figuring to find Native Americans selling blankets and turquoise trinkets, as they do where northern Arizona and New Mexico collide with southern Utah and Colorado. You can't even drive into this wedge of unsullied mountain land, where the borders of three states come together at altitudes of 3,000 to 4,000 feet. To experience the 8,274-acre rocky, woodsy terrain, you'll have to cinch up your boots, strap on a backpack, and trek in from trailheads on Highway 28 and the South Carolina side of the Chattooga River. Sorry, you'll have to leave your horses, bikes, and motorized vehicles in the parking area. Once you've breached the wilderness, feast your senses on Edenesque plant communities. Numerous rare and endangered plants flourish along a network of trails. The 3.5-mile Ellicott Rock Trail takes you up, up, and up a steep mountainside to a surveyor's rock marking the intersection of Georgia and the two Carolinas. Evergreen forests are thick with rhododendron, mountain laurel, and a nature book full of wildflowers. Look closely and you'll spot white-tailed deer, raccoons, birds of all sorts, and signs of elusive bobcats, bears, and coyotes. Majestic waterfalls plunge down the mountainsides. The National Wild and Scenic Chattooga River, made famous by the 1970s Burt Reynolds and Jon Voight movie, *Deliverance,* runs through the wilderness, with a goodly population of eastern brook trout you can sizzle at primitive campsites inside the wilderness and at developed campgrounds on the peripheries. For information contact the U.S. Forest Service's Clayton, Georgia, office; (706) 782–3320; www.fs.fed.us/conf.

Where Wallenda Walked on Air
Tallulah Gorge

On July 18, 1970, sixty-five-year-old Karl Wallenda took a walk across Tallulah Gorge. While 35,000 persons collectively held their breath (and a few rude yahoos snickered and wisecracked), the patriarch of the "Flying Wallendas" trapeze family stepped onto a 1¹¹⁄₁₆-inch steel cable strung 700 feet across the 1,200-foot-deep chasm. Eyes fixed straight ahead, he nimbly walked heel-to-toe, balancing a 36-foot pole. A third of the way across, he placed the pole carefully on the cable and executed a graceful handstand, waving his upturned feet at the cheering crowd. Two-thirds of the way, a second handstand was dedicated "to the boys in Vietnam." Wallenda pocketed $10,000 for his eighteen min-

How the mighty have fallen! The Great Wallenda was literally on top of the world when he walked across Tallulah Gorge in the 1970s. His luck, and pluck, ran out eight years later when he slipped from a high-wire strung between two ten-story hotels in San Juan, Puerto Rico.

utes of fame, which set a new record for cable height. Looking back on his stroll, he later said: "I think I want to look down, but I think I better not." Steel towers at the north and south ends of the gorge are the only physical evidence of his feat. His pluck ran out on March 22, 1978, when he fell to his death from a cable strung between two ten-story hotels in San Juan, Puerto Rico. You can read all about his walk at Tallulah Point Overlook, a privately owned snack bar and kitsch shop. Grab a Nehi grape soda and a bag of pork rinds and gape at the gorge from the covered porch. Oooo-eee! It's on Historic US 441 in the town of Tallulah Falls; (706) 754–4318; www.tallulahpoint.com.

Just up the highway, the Jane Hurt Yarn Interpretive Center in Tallulah Gorge State Park has a display on Wallenda's walk (including his gold-fringed, powder-blue costume). Also visit the Helen Dortch Longstreet Trail System around the gorge rim and into the gorge, and a sixty-three-acre lake with campsites. Periodically Georgia Power opens the dam's floodgates, bringing the South's Niagara briefly back to life. Kayakers, on your marks! Phone (706) 754–7970 or (800) 864–PARK or visit www.gastateparks.org.

The Host for the Games of the Winter Olympiad Will Be . . . The City of Dillard

Dillard

Atlanta hosted the 1996 Summer Olympics, so perhaps the Rabun County village of Dillard (population a few hundred) should bid for a future Winter Games. Some of the facilities are already in place. Sky Valley Resort, in this farthest northeast Georgia corner, is the most southerly ski resort in the whole United States. At an oxygen-thin elevation of 3,500 feet, Sky Valley's longest run is a dizzying half-mile, with a vertical drop of 250 feet and five bunny-to-advanced trails.

To complement nature's bounty, the resort manufactures its own powder from mid-December to mid-March. Snow bunnies and Olympic hopefuls should phone ahead for conditions (706–746–5303, www.skyvalley .com), which even in mid-winter can be more conducive to water-skiing on mountain lakes. (It's the global warming thing, don't you know.)

For après-ski unwinding, sit by the lodge fireplaces, play eighteen on Sky Valley's roller-coaster course, or hit the antiques malls on Dillard's US 441 strip. Then stuff yourselves stupid at the family-style tables at the renowned Dillard House, (706) 746–5348.

Where's the Bullion?
Washington

Whatever became of the Confederate gold? Was part of it once stored in the big iron chest that sits in the foyer of Washington's Mary Willis Library? The mystery has tantalized historians since May 24, 1865, when the gold vanished without a trace. Valued at $500,000 in 1865, and millions today, the gold was in a wagon train on its way from a Washington bank to banks in Virginia when armed raiders hijacked the shipment at a rural campsite in Lincoln County, Georgia. Whoever took it made a clean getaway, and over the decades "The Legend of the Lost Confederate Gold" has enticed slews of fortune hunters, all to no avail.

The mystery got new life in 1902, when a trunk thought to have once contained some of the fortune was found in the basement of a demolished Washington bank—the very same building where Jefferson Davis conducted the last meeting of the Confederate States Cabinet on May 5, 1865. The chest was donated to the Mary Willis Library in 1928, and in 1948 Atlanta locksmith Alvin Downs was asked to open it and, hopefully, discover the lost loot.

Atlanta Journal reporter Andrew Sparks witnessed the "Geraldo Rivera–esque" drama, as Downs spent an hour and half trying to decipher the chest's unique lock, which he described as a "tamper-proof, burglar-proof iron safe, immune from all but the most expert hands." Downs quickly discovered that the ornate, egg-shaped lock case on the front of the chest was a dummy. The real lock was in a hole in the top, through which children and curious adults would try to peek inside. The hole at one time had been camouflaged with an iron band, and Downs said that the key that fit the lock had to have been almost a foot long.

"As he worked at the opening, you could hear the tempered twang of his metal pick twisting in the lock," Sparks wrote with mounting you-are-there excitement. "The rusty catches under the old iron lid pulled back slightly as the pick turned, but the chest would not open. He loosened his tie and shucked his coat. He mopped sweat off his forehead as he hammered on the edges of the lid. With a crowbar, he pried up one corner; a rivet popped off the top and landed across the room. The locksmith worked his picks again and forced the crowbar, and suddenly the top was free."

Oh, if only this old iron chest could talk! It might be able to tell us the whereabouts of the Confederate gold it purportedly once held. Alas, it sits silent and empty in the foyer of the Mary Willis Library in Washington, tantalizing treasure hunters who believe the cache is still out there, waiting for them to discover it.

While onlookers held their breath, Downs lifted the lid and looked inside. In the bottom of the chest was an iron plate that had fallen from the lid. Then the treasure itself was sighted—a 1929 nickel mischievous little boys had dropped through the lock hole. Undaunted, there are still those who swear that the gold is hidden somewhere around Washington, waiting for a lucky soul to unearth it.

Gold or no gold, the Mary Willis Library is a treasure in its own right. Georgia's first free public library, the redbrick high-Victorian landmark with its stately round tower, was founded in 1888 by Dr. Francis T. Willis in honor of his daughter, Mary. Her likeness is the focus of a spectacular Tiffany Studios stained-glass window that may be more valuable than all the gold the old iron chest once held.

The Mary Willis Library is at 204 East Liberty Street, a block from the courthouse square in downtown Washington, the first municipality named for the Father of Our Country. It's open Monday through Saturday. Call (706) 678–7736.

While you're in town, you can't help being dazzled by dozens of white-columned antebellum homes, some of them quite spectacular. The most famous is the Robert Toombs House State Historic Site (216 East Robert Toombs Avenue; 706–678–4902; www.gastateparks.org). A wealthy planter and attorney, Toombs was a leader of Georgia's secession from the Union. Denied the Confederate presidency, he served as secretary of state under Jefferson Davis, whom he despised. After Appomattox he went abroad to thumb his nose at the oath of allegiance to the United States and died "The Unreconstructed Rebel."

JEANNETTE RANKIN, FIRST LADY OF THE U.S. CONGRESS

Jeannette Rankin was born in Montana and educated in New York. Montana sent her to Congress in 1917 as that male bastion's first female representative. In 1919 she was one of fifty members of Congress to naysay the Great War with Kaiser Wilhelm. In the face of national outrage over Pearl Harbor, Rep. Rankin voted against war with Japan in 1941. For the rest of her life, she marshaled pacifist forces against all conflicts, foreign and domestic. So what does she have to do with Georgia?

To take a breather from the national glare, she bought land in Oconee County in the 1920s and 1930s and turned an old farmhouse into "Shady Grove," her seasonal residence from the 1930s to the 1970s. An apartment complex now sits on the site. In the 1960s, Rankin built a circular house, known locally as the Roundhouse, as a retirement home for elderly women. The mission failed, and it's now a private home. Rankin died in California in 1973, but she's still got her pacifist eyes trained on Congress—in 1985 the state of Montana placed her statue in the U.S. Capitol's Statuary Hall.

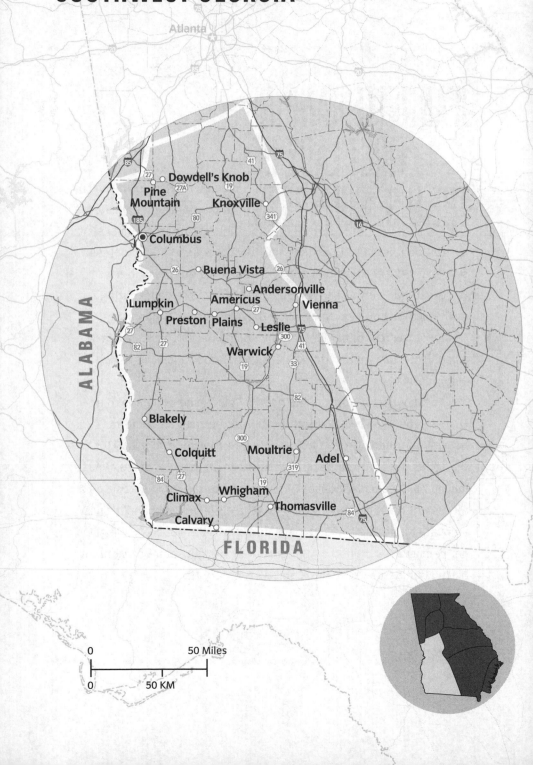

SOUTHWEST GEORGIA

Atlanta

ALABAMA

FLORIDA

Dowdell's Knob
Pine Mountain
Knoxville
Columbus
Buena Vista
Andersonville
Americus
Vienna
Lumpkin
Preston
Plains
Leslie
Warwick
Blakely
Colquitt
Moultrie
Adel
Climax
Whigham
Calvary
Thomasville

0   50 Miles

0   50 KM

SOUTHWEST GEORGIA

Franklin Delano Roosevelt, James Earl Carter, "Ma" Rainey, and St. EOM of Pasaquan are among the dramatis personae that color this large, diverse region that bumps against Alabama on the west and flows south with the Chattahoochee River from Atlanta's exurbs to the boggy Florida border. Butterflies are free at Callaway Gardens. Providence Canyon State Park may remind you a teeny bit of Arizona's Grand Canyon. Pasaquan, at Buena Vista, is one part Tibet, and the rest one man's vision. Carson McCullers cut her literary teeth on plays for her Columbus school chums before achieving lasting fame as author of *The Heart Is a Lonely Hunter* and *The Member of the Wedding*. Southwest Georgia's fecund fields nourished the peanut farmer who became president. To boost your energy while you're trying to see it all, knock back a mess of chitlins at Climax Swine Time and a brace of Scrambled Dogs at Columbus's Dinglewood Pharmacy with a Lumpy Coke.

When the Buzzards Come Back to Reed Bingham

Adel

As sure as the swallows wing back to California's Mission San Juan Capistrano in the spring, buzzards come home to Reed Bingham State Park, near Adel (pronounced "a-DELL"), each December. Their arrival is heralded by hundreds of gawking humans, who turn out for "Buzzard Day" nature talks, bird walks, and other fun stuff the first Saturday of December. If you can't make their homecoming party, you can view the homely vultures until they fly off again in early spring. The park's two types—turkey and black—roost in plain sight in the trees on the swampy banks of the Little River, which flows through the park into a 375-acre lake. As many as 5,000 buzzards bask in the warm south Georgia sunshine, soar on air currents with wings spread 6 feet wide, and generally have as big a time as is possible for their kind to have. Why do they come here? "I don't know; they just do, always have," a park ranger says. What do they eat? "Road kill mostly." Are children and pets in peril? "Not unless they're real small and don't move for a spell."

Reed Bingham State Park is on Highway 37, 6 miles west of Adel. While you keep an eye out for the buzzards, enjoy the park's camp sites, picnic pavilions, and summertime swimming beach. Call (229) 896–3551 or (800) 864–PARK or visit wwwgastateparks.org.

Lindy's First Solo

Americus

In 1923, four years before he captured the world's heart with his trans-Atlantic solo flight, an unheralded barnstormer named Charles A. Lindbergh purchased his first airplane, a single-engine World War I–surplus "Jenny," at Souther Field, a U.S. Army aviation training camp at Americus. "The Lone Eagle" took his Jenny on a test run over southwest Georgia, his first-ever solo. It was obviously love at first flight. How ya gonna keep 'em down on the farm after they've seen Sumter County? He attests to his feat on a plaque at what's now Americus airport: " I had not soloed up to the time I bought my Jenny at Americus, Georgia. (signed) Charles A. Lindbergh." Contact the Americus Welcome Center toll-free at (888) 278–6837 or visit www.therealgeorgia.com.

War Criminal or Scapegoat?

Andersonville

A granite obelisk honoring Capt. Henry Wirz is southwest Georgia's way of thumbing its nose at a military tribunal, which hanged Wirz in 1865 for "murder in violation of the laws of war" while he was commandant of the notorious Andersonville Prison. Under the Swiss-born Wirz's watch, thousands of Union Army prisoners of war died of starvation and disease. His supporters—unfortunately for him, Southerners, who'd forfeited their political clout—claimed that the camp's horrible conditions were beyond Wirz's control and that Confederate prisoners fared just as badly in Northern camps. But Northern outrage was such that Wirz was made to pay the price, the only man on either side convicted and executed for war crimes.

Wirz's angry ghost is said to still wander the old stockade, seeking a pardon for his part in one of America's greatest human tragedies. His monument is in Andersonville Civil War Village, across Highway 49 from the Andersonville National Historic Site and the National Prisoner of War Museum, which opened in 1998. Contact the Andersonville Civil War Village Welcome Center at (229) 924–2558 or visit www .andersonvillega.freeservers.com.

He was just following orders. So said those who put up a monument to Captain Henry Wirz, commandant of the notorious Andersonville Prison, where thousands of Union Army prisoners died of disease and starvation. Wirz was hanged for war crimes, but his supporters contend that the camp's deplorable conditions were beyond his control.

Providence Spring

Andersonville

Was it a miracle or merely an accident of nature? For the Andersonville Prison's tens of thousands of Union POWs, the only source of water was a small creek used for drinking, laundry, washing, and latrine. The summer of 1864 was hellishly hot and dry, and the POWs prayed for rain. On August 13 their prayers were answered with a downpour that flushed out the contaminated creek. During the storm a fierce bolt of lightning allegedly struck the ground, and from it sprang a clear, clean spring that's been flowing ever since. The granite Providence Spring House was built in 1901 by the Women's Relief Corps.

Andersonville National Historic Site and Cemetery, on Highway 49, 10 miles north of Americus, is open daily. Free admission. Call (229) 924–0343 or visit www.nps.gov/ande.

A clear, clean spring inside the Providence Spring House was the answer to Union POWs' prayers. In August 1863, the prisoners prayed for rain to relieve their suffering. As if in response, a downpour cleared a polluted stream and delivered fresh water that continues to flow.

The Last Woody

Blakely

The wooden Confederate flagpole, stationed on the Early County Court-house lawn in Blakely since Georgia seceded in 1861, is the last remaining Confederate flagpole still standing. The postage stamp–sized Confederate battle emblem tagged onto a string of decommissioned flags at the tail end of Georgia's new state flag is the old pole's last tribute to the Lost Cause. You can salute the flag in front of the courthouse, on Highway 62 a mile from U.S. Highway 27, about 80 miles south of Columbus.

St. EOM of Pasaquan

Buena Vista

In New York and other worldly places, Eddie Owens Martin blended right in with the exotic wallpaper. In Buena Vista (BEW-na Vista), Georgia, population 1,500, circa the 1950s, Eddie stood out like a cockatoo in a barnyard. Born to dirt-poor sharecroppers in 1908, Eddie was fourteen when he heard voices from the spirit world telling him, "You're gonna be the start of something new, and you're gonna be called a Pasaquoyan and your name will be St. EOM" (his initials, pronounced like the Eastern chant "om").

Eddie did some research and discovered that "pasa" means "pass" in Spanish and "quoyan" is an Oriental term for bringing the past and future together. There wasn't much calling for Pasaquoyans around Buena Vista—folks were lots more concerned about rainfall, pork bellies and the peanut crop, and getting to the Baptist church on time—so off Eddie went to New York, where he found employment as a street hustler, waiter, bartender, and Tarot card reader. He traveled the earth's far ends, and in the late 1950s returned home to Buena Vista. On his family's former farmland, he and his male partner created an amazing art environment called Land of Pasaquan.

Driving up the dirt road, five minutes from Buena Vista's square, and suddenly beholding Pasaquan, you feel like Dorothy swirling through the sepia-toned tornado and stepping out into the Technicolor Land of Oz. Looking for all the world like a misplaced piece of Tibet or Angkor Wat, the cosmic-colored concrete, wood, wire, sheet metal, and aluminum compound is covered with symbols of cultures light-years removed from rural Georgia. Encircled by a zig-zag psychedelic wall are mystical faces; totemic statues taller than the tallest man, with protruding noses and all-seeing eyes; whirling patterns of circles and stripes; grinning snakes; pinwheels; mandalas; moons, suns, and stars; pagodalike temples; and a circular sand pit where Eddie and his companion danced and chanted.

Is this Tibet or Marion County? The late Eddie Owens Martin (a.k.a. St. EOM of Pasaquan) created these exotic Himalayan-looking totems, grinning snakes, pinwheels, mandalas, moons, suns, stars, and pagoda-like temples on his farmland near Buena Vista, the Marion County seat.

To finance his creativity (saints have to eat, too), Eddie donned flowing robes, a candy-striped turban, feathered headdresses, jingly
bracelets, and bells and told fortunes and sold jewelry on the courthouse square in Buena Vista. Since his death at age seventy-seven, in
1986, volunteers and preservationists from the Columbus Museum of
Art, 30 miles from Buena Vista, have restored the compound and welcome visitors, particularly those who show up with buckets of paint and
elbow grease. As you're wandering, pondering how on earth such an
other-worldly place ended up among the peanut fields and God-fearing
folk of Marion County, Georgia, bear in mind these words from St. EOM:
"I built this place to have something to identify with. Here I can be in my
own world, with my temples and designs and the spirit of God. I can
have my own spirits and my own thoughts."

Contact the Marion County/Buena Vista Chamber of Commerce at
(800) 647–2842 or (229) 649–2842.

Mule Day, Mule Day
Calvary

Mule Day, held in Calvary on the first Saturday of November, salutes
these stalwart ships of the cornfields. Hundreds of jacks and jennies
cross through Calvary, on Highway 11, a mule-flop toss from the Florida
border. Ribbons are bestowed for beauty, poise, congeniality, and
cussedness. Mules go haunch to haunch in a plowing contest. Not to
be outshone, two-legged critters show off their artistry at cane grinding, corn shucking, quilting, syrup making, a tobacco spittin' competition, and the mule chitlins supper (just kidding, just kidding). For
information, contact the Bainbridge-Decatur County Chamber of Commerce at (229) 246–4774 or visit www.bainbridgega.com/chamber.

Days of Swine and Roses

Climax

Stash that leftover turkey, baby girl! It's Climax Swine Time. Since 1975 pork disciples from as far off as southeast Alabama and northwest Florida have flocked to Decatur County's big pig party, held the week-end after Thanksgiving. For two days Climax, a hamlet linked by U.S. Highway 84 to Bainbridge, the county seat, pays homage to the hog's esteemed place in southwest Georgia history, economy, and culture. And they have themselves one heck of a swell time, beginning with a sausage-and-all-the-trimmings breakfast at the Chitlins Barn.

Would you like fries or coleslaw with your chitlins? At Climax Swine Time, the Saturday after Thanksgiving, chitlins and every other part of the pig are part of a celebration that hails the hog's esteemed place in the hearts of southwest Georgians.

(What are chitlins, you ask? There's no delicate way to say it. Properly called chitterlings, they're pork intestines, chopped into bite-size pieces, boiled and fried, and eaten by the mess—a "mess" being a heaping portion of something ambrosial; e.g., turnips, collards, taters, pork chops, or chitlins. If you'd like to take the plunge, first douse your mess with hellfire hot sauce, then shut your eyes and try to block out the origin of what you're eating, like you do with escargots and lamb chops. Chew fast and swallow hard, with a big glass of gum-aching sweet tea. I once heard a devotee of the dish explain, "You can tell you have a good mess of chitlins if you find some corn still inside 'em.").

Miss Swine Time and Junior Miss Swine Time lead a festive parade. Old-timers dressed up like Minnie Pearl and Grandpa Jones put on a Grand Ole Opry show. Nimbler folks trot around town in the Swine Time 5,000-meter run. Then come the main events: the dressed-up pig judging (hog warts and all); eating-the-chitlins; the hog calling contest; corn shucking; turkey calling; clogging (square dancing with heavy metal taps on your shoes that cause a racket like July 4 fireworks); the pig parade; and the greased-pig chase. For the grand finale the honorees make the ultimate sacrifice—they come to the barbecue supper chopped, sliced, hammed, and ribbed, basted in the festive sauces of the season.

For more information on these down-to-earth events, contact the Bainbridge-Decatur County Chamber of Commerce; (229) 246–4774; www.bainbridgega.com/chamber.

Dr. Blue
Colquitt

Many colorful characters are highlighted in the "Swamp Gravy" series of musical folklife plays performed in March and October by talented people of Colquitt and Miller County. One of the most "colorful" was Dr. W. C. Hays. "In the early 1940s," says Charlotte Philipps, director of the historical museum inside the Swamp Gravy Theater on Colquitt's courthouse square, "Dr. Hays treated his throat infection with silver nitrate, which was a popular remedy at the time. Unbeknownst to him, Dr. Hays was allergic to silver nitrate, which turned his skin a very distinctive shade of blue for the rest of his life. When I painted a mannequin of Dr. Hays for the museum, an old friend of his said I'd gotten it just about right and that the doctor might even have been a bit darker blue." If you'd like to see Dr. Blue and other colorful personalities, contact Swamp Gravy—Georgia's Official Folklife Play; (229) 758–5450; www.swampgravy.com. Colquitt is on US 27, about 90 miles south of Columbus.

Colquitt's Storytelling Walls
Colquitt

"If these walls could talk," isn't wishful thinking in Colquitt. Walk around the town square, and five bigger-than-life murals, created by the Colquitt/Miller County Arts Council's Millennium Mural Project, "speak" about events that have shaped the lives of the peanut-farming community of 2,500. "Bull Comes to Colquitt" is one of four panels of Saturday on the Square, by Alabama artist Wes Hardin. In the 1920s a big brown-and-white bull frequently took a notion to come to town and socialize. Workmen at a sawmill on the edge of the square would sound the alarm: "Bull's out! Mr. Johnnie's bull's coming! Everybody get outta the way!"

Neighbors help out an ailing farmer's family in this mural in downtown Colquitt. It's one of five large wall paintings that depict scenes that have shaped the lives of the community of 2,500. Others show a runaway bull, young men going off to war, and teenagers doing what teenagers do best, standing on a corner, watching all the girls go by.

Pedestrians would run for cover, and merchants would clear their goods from the sidewalks. Before the bull could lay waste to all the "china shops" in town, "Mr. Johnnie" would show up and lead his wayfaring bovine back home—until the next time. Other scenes depict neighbors coming to tend an ailing farmer's fields; local boys leaving home to fight in World War II; and 1950s teenagers standing on the corner, watching all the girls go by.

Ma Rainey's House
Columbus

"Empress of the Blues" Ma Rainey (née Gertrude Pridgett) began her flamboyant life in 1886 in the workaday Chattahoochee River textile mill city of Columbus. Her minstrel show parents pushed little Gertrude into the streets and honky-tonks at a tender age, where she grew up real fast. She was eighteen when she married Will Rainey and hit the road with his Rabbit Foot Minstrels. A quick study, she found her own "voice," ditched Rainey and the granny-sounding "Gertrude," and blazed a thirty-year career as "Mother of the Blues."

Ma's most celebrated "child" was Bessie Smith. The future "Queen of the Blues" was a teenager when Ma discovered her in 1920, hoofing and singing for handouts on Chattanooga street corners. She also boosted the careers of such up-and-coming musicians as Louis "Satchmo" Armstrong and Georgia-born Fletcher Henderson.

One of the earliest female recording stars, Ma made ninety-four blues discs before 1928—more than forty-five were her own compositions. She flamed out in 1934 and went home to Columbus. She died in 1939 in her modest house at 805 Fifth Avenue and was buried in nearby Porterdale Cemetery. Her former two-story frame house, listed on the National Register of Historic Places, is a stop—viewed from the outside—on the Columbus Black Heritage Tour. Columbusites hope one day to turn the vacant house into a tribute to Ma Rainey and her music. Like a big wheel, the honors still keep on turning. In 1993 she received the Georgia Woman of Achievement Award and was inducted into the Georgia Music Hall of Fame. In 1994 she joined Elvis, Satchmo, Duke Ellington, and other music immortals as the star of her own "Ma Rainey, Mother of the Blues" postage stamp. Get tour information from the Columbus Convention & Visitors Bureau; (800) 999–1613; www .columbusga.com.

Gertrude "Ma" Rainey left this Columbus house to find fame and fortune as "Empress of the Blues." She made nearly one hundred blues recordings, discovered Bessie Smith, and worked with Louis Armstrong and Georgia-born Fletcher Henderson. When she died in 1939, she was buried in Columbus's Porterdale Cemetery. Her former home is a stop on the Columbus Black Heritage Tour.

"AF-LAC!"

The obstreperous duck who's become the most famous commercial icon since the "Where's the beef?" lady pops up in bedrooms, roller coasters, Yogi Berra's barbershop, parks, golf courses, airport concourses, and race tracks, honking "AF-LAC!" to the uninitiated, who don't realize their critical need for supplemental insurance. When he needs R&R from the limelight, the AF-LAC duck comes home to the American Family Life Assurance Corporation's headquarters near downtown Columbus. Sorry, no autographs or private audiences. But if you hear a loud honk under your bed some night, or trip over loose poultry while racing for your flight, grab your pen and paper.

No Place like Home
Columbus

An historic marker in front of the tidy white bungalow at 1519 Stark Avenue, in the middle-class Wildwood neighborhood, commemorates novelist Carson McCullers (1917–67), who spent her childhood and later years here. Little Lula Carson Smith wanted to be a concert pianist when she grew up, but she spent so much of her childhood reading books and writing and performing skits that by the time she did reach maturity, the future author of *The Member of the Wedding* and *The Heart Is a Lonely Hunter* was a hopeless captive of the writing muse. In a 1948 magazine article, "How I Began to Write," she recalled penning and producing plays, usually featuring her mother and sisters in leading roles and her neighbors as audience and critics.

"They were eclectic," she said, "from hashed-over Shakespeare to shows I made up and wrote down in my nickel Big Chief notebooks."

Out of sync with her schoolmates, who taunted the bookish Carson as odd and freaky, she wasn't seriously courted until the summer of 1935, when she met Reeves McCullers, a soldier stationed at nearby Fort Benning. The young infantryman won over Carson's mother with flowers and candy, and she gave her blessing to her daughter's marriage in the Stark Avenue garden. Big mistake, Mom. Bride and groom were both bisexual, frequently attracted to the same man or woman (which precipitated no end of marital warfare). Reeves eventually committed suicide, and Carson returned to Columbus to care for her widowed mother. They sold the Stark Avenue house and moved to Nyack, New York, where Carson died in 1967. The house is privately owned and not open to visitors.

Get tour information from the Columbus Convention & Visitors Bureau; (800) 999–1613; www.columbusga.com.

CARSON McCULLER
—— 1917 - 1967 ——

The family of author Carson McCullers moved to this in 1927. Here Lula Carson Smith spent her formative years and here she began to write. putting on shows in the two rooms. using the sliding doors as curtains and drafting Lamar and sister Rita as actors. Shows grew into plays. and novels. She left to study writing in New York in 1934. a teacher told her that the best stories can be found i own back yard. her "green arcade" of trees drew her home In the summer of 1935 she met James Reeves McCullers, Jr., she married in the garden here in Sept., 1937. They m North Carolina where the young author completed her firs The Heart Is a Lonely Hunter. During World War II. with overseas. Carson lived in New York but often returned home and rest. She liked to sit in the kitchen. absorbing its the aroma of food cooking and the conversation of th In her front bedroom she kept her piano and the typewrite she worked on her novel. and later prize-winning play. Th of the Wedding. After the death of her father in 1944. and her mother made their home in Nyack. N.Y.

THIS MARKER ERECTED BY THE FRIENDS OF CARSON McCULLERS, INC.

ISIDOR STRAUSS, BLOCKADE RUNNER

In 1863 Columbus importer/exporter Lloyd Bowers and his eighteen-year-old secretary, Isidor Strauss, joined a group of Georgia and Virginia entrepreneurs in a scheme to run their merchandise through the Union blockade of Southern ports. Strauss and other members went to England, where they contracted for construction of three shallow-draft blockade runners. When the ships were built, Strauss remained in England as the company's foreign agent. After the war he and his family moved to New York City, where he became sole owner of Macy's department stores in 1896. In 1912 Strauss and his wife, Ida, perished on the *Titanic*.

Author of *The Member of the Wedding* and *The Heart Is A Lonely Hunter*, Lula Carson Smith McCullers began her turbulent life in a Columbus house where this historic marker stands.

LUMPY COKE

Folks in other parts of the country have no doubt experienced the exotic taste of a cherry-flavored, lemon, or vanilla Coke. But unless you've sojourned in Southwest Georgia's Peanut Country, you're probably a stranger to the gastronomic rush of a "Lumpy Coke," which blends goobers with one of the state's other celebrated products. Here's the recipe:

1 bottle or can Coca-Cola (usually called Coke or Co-Coler in these parts)

1 generous handful shelled Georgia peanuts. (Don't try this with peanuts from Alabama, Texas, or any other place.)

Open Co-Coler, take two to four swallows, and set aside. Scoop peanuts into one hand, grasp drink bottle or can with the other, and gently pour the peanuts into the beverage. Turn up the container and drink heartily.

Some folks like to shake the mixture before drinking to "settle" the fizz created by the chemistry of the salty nuts and carbonation. If you use Columbus's own RC (Royal Crown) Cola instead of Coke, you're entitled to enjoy it with a MoonPie.

Coca-Cola's Birthplace

Columbus

Atlanta claims to be the birthplace of Coca-Cola, but the world's most famous soft drink actually evolved from a formula concocted in Dr. John Stith Pemberton's apothecary in Columbus. Dr. Pemberton reportedly dispensed the drink's forerunner at a Columbus soda fountain but didn't perfect it until he moved to Atlanta after the Civil War. In 1888 he sold the formula to Asa Candler for $1,750. Pemberton lived long enough to see Candler's marketing wizardry turn his simple drink into a worldwide phenomenon. Kept in a vault at an Atlanta bank, the formula is one of the corporate world's best-kept secrets.

Two marble-topped soda fountains and an array of Coca-Cola memorabilia are in the apothecary behind Pemberton's Columbus house. The Greek Revival house, where Pemberton's family lived from 1855 to 1860, has family furnishings and an oil portrait of Dr. Pemberton in the parlor.

Pemberton House, 11 Seventh Street, is maintained by the Historic Columbus Foundation, which offers daily tours. Call (706) 322–0756 or visit www.historiccolumbus.com.

Made-in-Georgia Ironclad

Columbus

Columbus is 100 miles from the open waters of the Gulf of Mexico, but in the mid-nineteenth century it was one of the South's busiest shipbuilding centers. In December 1864 workmen at the Columbus Shipyards were putting the final touches on the iron-ram CSS *Jackson* and preparing to put the 225-foot vessel into action. But before the ironclad battlecraft hit the muddy waters of the Chattahoochee, Union raiders crossed the river from Alabama and burned her to the waterline.

The hull drifted 30 miles downriver and sank to the bottom, where it rested until salvagers pulled it up in the 1960s. Until February 2001 the *Jackson*'s huge wooden beams and iron propellers were displayed in a cramped outdoor shed at the James Woodruff Naval Museum. Now the ship's remains are the star attraction at the new 40,000-square foot Port Columbus Civil War Naval Museum, near downtown Columbus.

You view the hull from a platform above the bow and at floor level. Only about one-third of the original ship, weighing around 560,000 pounds, is on display. That's without its twin layers of iron plate, six guns—the lightest weighing 10,000 pounds—and two engines that weighed 30,000 pounds each. A steel "ghost" structure built over the hull gives a sense of the ship's immense size and raises the question: How in the world were they going to maneuver this whopping big boat through the narrow banks of the Chattahoochee? About one hundred pieces of the ship's plating and one of its 7-inch Brooke rifles are exhibited at a re-creation of the Columbus Shipyards, outside the main museum building.

The museum's hundreds of other exhibits include remnants of the CSS *Chattahoochee*, a built-in-Columbus wooden warship also scuttled by Yankee raiders, and a partial replica of the USS *Hartford*, the flagship that Union Admiral David Farragaut rode into Mobile Bay, shouting the immortal words, "Damn the torpedoes, full speed ahead!"

The Port Columbus Civil War Naval Museum is at 1002 Victory Drive, Columbus. Call (706) 327–9798 or visit www.portcolumbus.org. Admission fee.

Franklin, My Dear
Dowdell's Knob

When the pressures of World War II caused the walls of the Little White House at Warm Springs to squeeze around him, Franklin Roosevelt got in his hand-controlled 1938 Ford convertible and sought solitude in the countryside. One of his favorite retreats was Dowdell's Knob, a rocky 1,395-foot spur of the Pine Mountain ridge, with panoramic vistas of the green, rolling Pine Mountain Valley. According to local lore, he was enjoying the view one morning when a grizzled farmer wandered up the rough road and marveled at finding the president and his Ford.

Even presidents need their space. When he wanted his, President Franklin Roosevelt cranked up his '38 Ford ragtop and drove himself out to Dowdell's Knob, on Pine Mountain. Sometimes he'd bring along some friends and have a picnic on the grounds, with linen napery and fine china, of course.

THIS WAS HIS GEORGIA

Franklin D. Roosevelt was a frequent visitor (41 trips) to Warm Springs from 1924-1945. Dowdell's Knob was one of his favorite spots for both quiet contemplation and picnics. F.D.R. visited this spot overlooking Pine Mountain Valley as a private citizen, as governor of New York and as 32nd president of the U.S.

He wanted more people to visit the area and urged the building of the scenic highway across Pine Mt. and the construction of the spur here (1937).

President Roosevelt had the grill built to help him enjoy picnics in his more formal style. He preferred linen-draped tables with hot dishes served from silver. In place of a blanket he preferred to sit on a chair or on an automobile seat placed on the ground.

F.D.R. came here to contemplate the upcoming founding of the United Nations and the Americans dying on Okinawa and in Germany during his final trip to Warm Springs, April, 1945.

072-7   GEORGIA HISTORIC MARKER   1984

"How'd you get that car up here?" he asked. FDR replied that the road was rough, but the view was worth the bumps. He predicted that some day many others would come to appreciate the area's rugged beauty. The pragmatic old farmer wasn't convinced: "Ask me, this mountain ain't good for nothing but running hogs on," he harrumphed.

The two shook hands, and Roosevelt invited the man to visit him at the Little White House. Roosevelt made his last visit to Dowdell's Knob on April 10, 1945. Two days later he died while sitting for his portrait, which sits unfinished in the Little White House.

Dowdell's Knob is off Highway 190 inside 9,047-acre FDR State Park, the state's largest public park. The road's been paved since FDR's last visit, and picnic tables and grills come with the views he loved so much. A historic marker called "This Was His Georgia" notes that he fostered construction of the scenic highway across Pine Mountain and the spur road to the knob. Even in this rustic setting, FDR couldn't forgo his aristocratic Hyde Park upbringing: "He had the grill built to help him enjoy picnics in his more formal style. He preferred linen-draped tables with hot dishes served on silver. In place of a blanket on the ground, he preferred to sit in a chair or on an automobile car seat placed on the ground." His namesake state park's amenities also include campsites, cottages, hiking, horseback riding, two fishing and boating lakes, and a swimming pool shaped like the Liberty Bell. Phone (706) 663–4858 or (800) 864–PARK or visit www.gastateparks.org.

The Lone Star Flag
Knoxville

Texans owe their proud Lone Star flag to a banner created by Joanna Troutman, a seventeen-year-old farm girl from Georgia's Crawford County. In 1835 the Georgia Battalion, a troop of volunteers, marched to the aid of Texas freedom fighters under Troutman's home-sewn flag—a pale blue field emblazoned with a single white star, with the words "Texas and Liberty" and a Latin verse that translates, "Where Liberty Dwells There Is My Country."

Three weeks after the Alamo, the troop met the Mexican army—and immortality—at the Presidio LaBahia, an old Spanish fortress near Goliad. The Presidio was under command of Col. James Walker Fannin of Columbus. When word arrived of an approaching Mexican army, Fannin abandoned the fortified Presidio and led his troops toward the nearby town of Victoria. They were trapped in an open field, soundly defeated, and marched back to the fort. On Palm Sunday, March 27, 1836, Fannin and 352 of his men were executed by firing squad. The death toll was nearly twice that at the Alamo, and "Remember the Alamo! Remember Goliad!" became a rallying cry of the Texas Revolution.

In 1986 historians Lee Basore of Austin, Texas, and Lillian Champion of Pine Mountain, Georgia, re-created the Georgia Battalion flag for the 150th anniversary of the Goliad Massacre. Blunderer or foiled strategist, Colonel Fannin lives on in the name of Georgia and Texas counties and the battlefield where he fell. Joanna Troutman lives on in the Lone Star flag of modern Texas. Her deed was honored and full rights of Texas citizenship conferred on her reinterment in Austin in 1915.

You can read all about it in the Old Knoxville Jail and Museum, on Highway 42 in Knoxville; (478) 836–3825; www.robertacrawford chamber.org.

PLEASING THE PRESIDENTIAL PALATE: CHICKEN COUNTRY CAPTAIN

The origins of Chicken Country Captain are lost in the mists of time. A long-ago cook no doubt came up with the idea of sparking her same-old, same-old Sunday chicken with spices, herbs, and vegetables. Succeeding generations added pinches of this and dashes of that and claimed the dish as their own invention. But Country Captain's most famous exponent was Daisy Bonner, who prepared it for President Franklin D. Roosevelt at the Little White House at Warm Springs. FDR couldn't get enough of it, and newspapers and magazines spread this gastronomic wonder into homes and restaurants from coast to coast. It's still served for special occasions in middle and southwest Georgia. It goes like this:

1 hen or 2 fryers

2 or 3 green peppers, chopped

2 or 3 garlic cloves, chopped

2 onions, chopped

1 can whole tomatoes

1 teaspoon curry powder, or more to taste

2 cups rice, boiled until dry

1 teaspoon thyme

¼ cup raisins, for the sauce

¼ cup raisins, to garnish top

¼ cup almonds or other nuts, for the sauce

¼ cup almonds or other nuts, for garnish

¼ cup sliced fresh mushrooms

Salt and pepper to taste

Accustomed to the grandeur of the White House and his family's mansion at Hyde Park, President Franklin Roosevelt felt more at home in the no-frills Little White House he built in the Georgia countryside. One of the things he liked best was Chicken Country Captain, a zesty dish created by his cook, Daisy Bonner. Eleanor sure never cooked like this.

Boil chicken until done, then debone. Make the sauce from the chopped green peppers, garlic, onions, tomatoes, mushrooms, almonds, raisins, thyme, salt, pepper, and curry powder. Add chicken and simmer on top of the stove or in a casserole in the oven at 325–350 degrees for one hour. Serve over rice. Garnish with chopped green pepper, raisins, and nuts.

Daisy complemented FDR's favorite dish with baked grapefruit, French-cut green beans, mixed green salad, fresh breads, and chocolate soufflé or Georgia peach cobbler. After FDR's death she left this penciled message on the kitchen woodwork: "Daisy Bonner cooked the first meal and last one in this cottage for President Roosevelt."

You can read it for yourself at the Little White House State Historic Site, 401 Little White House Road, Warm Springs; (706) 655–5870 or (800) 864–PARK; www.gastateparks.org. Admission fee.

Is This the Person with Whom I Am Speaking?

Leslie

You pull into Leslie (population 445) hoping to do no more than fill your tank and grab a few pecan logs at the convenience store. Before you leave town, you end up answering your kids' question: "Where do cell phones come from?" The Georgia Rural Telephone Museum traces today's ubiquitous portable phones all the way to 1876, when Alexander Graham Bell's liquid transmitter made history as the first device through which the human voice was sent.

In 1995 Tommy C. Smith, who owns southwest Georgia's Citizens Telephone Company, salvaged a 1911 cotton warehouse and opened one of the world's largest phone museums. Along with Bell's liquid transmitter, Smith's 2,000 pieces of telephonia include wooden voice boxes, early telephones of every size and description, the first pay telephone booths, and full-scale exhibits of switchboard operators in early-1900s dress (Sorry, Ernestine, the first operators were men). There's a model of Bell's workshop, a rare 1882 fifty-line switchboard, one of the first operator headsets (circa 1880), a 1900s Model A Ford service truck, picture phones, cell phones, and a model of TelStar, the first

Telephone lines were such a novelty in the early 1900s, many deer hunting sharpshooters couldn't resist the temptation to take a pop at them. This sign at the Georgia Rural Telephone Museum in Leslie appealed to the hunters' better side, often in vain.

"Is this the person with whom I am speaking? I sure hope so, because I can't make hide nor hair out of this confangled thing." It's one of the exhibits at the Georgia Rural Telephone Museum in Leslie.

communications satellite. A re-created Creek Indian village links smoke signals with today's communications. "Bubba the Bear" communicates with kids on a "private line." Since this is Jimmy Carter country, Smith acquired a portable White House switchboard that accompanied the president on his home stays at Plains. Dangling wire lines were targets some hot-fingered hunters couldn't resist, so a sign pleads: SPORTSMEN, PLEASE DON'T SHOOT AT THE TELEPHONE LINES.

The museum is on U.S. Highway 280, 135 Bailey Avenue, in Leslie, 22 miles west of Interstate 75 exit 101/Cordele and 12 miles east of Americus. Nominal charge. Phone (229) 874–4786 or visit www.sowega .net/~museum.

Georgia's Grand Canyon
Lumpkin

By all accounts it took the Colorado River millions of years to carve Arizona's Grand Canyon. By comparison southwest Georgia's Providence Canyon is the "instant grits" of the canyon kingdom. In the early 1800s the sixteen canyons that now form the 1,110-acre Providence Canyon State Park were flat, featureless piney woods. As settlers moved into the area, they cleared the trees to cultivate corn and other crops. As the trees fell, the loosely grained soil eroded and washed away. With little vegetation as a deterrent, rainwater ripped through the exposed terrain, tearing away big gashes. By the 1850s farmers and livestock were stumbling through ditches 3 to 5 feet deep. The pace quickened after the Civil War—poor cultivation methods continued, and the ditches grew into canyons now 150 feet from rim to bottom, half a mile long, and 300 feet across. Like the "big ditch" in Arizona, Providence Canyon is a geological primer, with layers of rock and soil in shades of pink, purple, tan, salmon, orange, and chalky white. With a little help from your imagination, you can see people, animals, and flowers in the formations standing alone in the canyons. The park interpretive center's slide show and exhibits will give you an overview before you set off to walk the rim and hike down to the canyon floor.

Providence Canyon, southwest Georgia's "Little Grand Canyon," is a textbook example of what a century and a half of runaway soil erosion can do to a few hundred acres of perfectly good farmland.

Backpackers who overnight on the backcountry trail are treated to the dazzling spectacle of sunrise and sunset on the canyon walls. Spring and fall visitors are rewarded with clusters of rare plumleaf azaleas and other vibrant wildflowers. Recoup your energy at the park's picnic tables, pavilions, and campsites. Providence Canyon State Park is open sunrise to sundown daily; parking fee. From Columbus take US 27/280 south to US 27 to Lumpkin, then follow Highway 39C for 7 miles west to the park entrance. Call (229) 838–6202 or (800) 864–PARK, or visit www.gastateparks.org.

OUCH! THAT SMARTS

This sign is posted on a Griffin roadway:

**IF YOU HIT THIS SIGN,
YOU HIT THIS BRIDGE.**

Don't say you weren't warned.

Moultrie's Little Elephant
Moultrie

When William F. Duggan was a boy in the early 1900s, he wanted to run off and join the circus. When he grew up, he did his dream one better— he owned a circus. When he died in 1950, his son commissioned a marble statue of Duggan's favorite baby elephant and placed it on his grave in Moultrie's Pleasant Grove Primitive Baptist Church cemetery. With its upturned trunk and ears like great big trumpets, the little pachyderm seems to still be answering his master's call to the big top. You can see him on Highway 37, east of Moultrie. For information contact the Moultrie-Colquitt County Chamber of Commerce; (229) 985–2131; www.moultriechamber.com.

I Heard an Owl Butterfly Call My Name
Pine Mountain

You step out of the sultry heat of a Georgia summer day, or the chill of a winter day, into a glass-enclosed rain forest that mimics the steamy Amazon. Whoa, Nelly! Before you can shuck your coat and get your bearings, butterflies are on your nose, in your hair, on your out stretched palms, and up your sleeves. Don't panic; they don't bite, and some folks think being used as a lepidopteran's landing strip portends good luck. (It's a sweet thought, but don't rush out for lottery tickets on the strength of it.) At any rate, they're everywhere you look. Flying clouds of fluttering ebony, ochre, scarlet, blue, jade, and magenta wings pose for photos, dart through the 12-foot waterfalls, nibble on oranges and overripe bananas, and park on you, the foliage, and the glass walls of the Cecil B. Day Butterfly Center at Callaway Gardens— then zoom away like the cartoon Jetsons. When your life span is a mere few days or weeks, you can't afford to stand still very long.

One of the oldest and largest tropical butterfly conservatories in North America, the Day Center was a gift from Mrs. Deen Day Smith in memory of her late husband, Cecil B. Day, founder of Days Inns of America. It was the first to incorporate butterflies with horticulture and the first anywhere in the world to showcase butterflies from Africa. Those share the octagon-shaped conservatory with upward of 1,000 freewheeling "flying flowers" from Costa Rica, Panama, Mexico, Malaysia, Brazil, and Taiwan, along with Georgia's homeboy varieties. Painted ladies, monarchs, blue morphos, tiger swallowtails, variegated fritillaries, and the other seventy-five or so species all have their admirers. My favorite is the owl butterfly (genus *caligoeurilochus*). As big as the hummingbirds that share its space, the Central American owl comes equipped with an ingenious bit of life-saving camouflage: At night, would-be predators mistake the big round black-and-yellow patch on its wings for the eye of barred, barn, or horned owl and pick on somebody else. During the day it's be hid or be lunch.

Before you leave the conservatory, do a body check for hitchhikers looking to flee their gilded cage. Around the outside of the center, one-and-a-half acres of gardens are planted to attract native butterflies and birds. Callaway Gardens horticulturists hold workshops for home gardeners who'd like their own yards to be butterfly-friendly.

Native leps wing freely through Callaway's 14,000 acres, where there are thirteen man-made lakes for swimming, boating, and fishing; hiking and biking trails; a birds of prey show; the world's largest azalea garden (showcasing the rare plumleaf azalea, otherwise found only in the wilds of west Georgia); the Lady Bird Johnson Wildflower Trail; golf and tennis; lodgings and dining rooms. The resort and nature sanctuary is just south of the town of Pine Mountain on US 27, 70 miles southwest of Atlanta airport and 30 miles north of Columbus. Phone (800) CALLAWAY or visit www.callawaygardens.com.

An owl butterfly finds a soft landing pad on the hand of a young lady visiting the Cecil B. Day Butterfly Center at Callaway Gardens. The Central American owl is one of seventy-five lepidopteran species that fly freely through the glass-walled conservatory, named for the founder of the Days Inns motel chain.

The Grinning Peanut
Plains

A peanut with an overactive thyroid and a famous toothsome grin welcomes visitors to Jimmy Carter's hometown of Plains. Made of wooden hoops, chicken wire, aluminum foil, and polyurethane, the 13-foot-tall goober, on Highway 45 a half mile north of town, was a gift to the town from friends of our thirty-ninth president. When termites took a liking to "Mr. Peanut" a few years back, townsfolk came to the rescue with patches of cement. Along with Jimmah himself, his peanutty icon is one of the Jimmy Carter National Historic Site's most popular photo ops. While you're in town, see the exhibits on Carter's life in the former Plains High School, visit the Carter Boyhood Home and farm where he grew up, and the train depot, where his 1976 presidential campaign was plotted. Contact the National Park Service; (229) 824–4104; www.nps.gov/jica.

Texas tourist Ann Ruff is dwarfed by a peanut with a famous toothy grin. The 13-foot goober welcomes visitors to former President Jimmy Carter's hometown of Plains, now a National Historic Site.

Zero-ing In
Preston

The white cupola atop the two-story, redbrick Webster County Court-house in Preston (population 2,200) was added in the wake of the December 7, 1941, Japanese attack on Pearl Harbor. Every night until V-E Day and V-J Day civil defense volunteers manned the cupola, on the look-out for Japanese Zeros approaching from the West Coast and the German Luftwaffe blitzkrieging from across the Atlantic. Eternal vigilance is the price of freedom, and Webster County's peanut and cotton fields sur-vived the war unscathed. Preston is on US 280, 8 miles west of Plains.

Lt. Henry Ossian Flipper
Thomasville

Henry Ossian Flipper is free at last. Born into slavery near Thomasville in 1856, Flipper became the first African-American graduate of the U.S. Military Academy at West Point twenty-one years later. For four years the newly minted second lieutenant served with distinction with the U.S. Cavalry's "Buffalo soldiers" on the western Plains. Then Flipper's world flip-flopped. In 1881 he was charged with, then exonerated of, embezzling government funds. However, he unwittingly dug himself a hole when he tried to replace the money with his own funds and look for the guilty culprit on his own. For that he was found guilty of "con-duct unbecoming an officer and a gentleman" and dishonorably dis-charged from the army. For the next forty-eight years, while he made a name for himself as an engineer and surveyor and as a special agent for the U.S. Justice Department and an interpreter for the Senate Commit-tee on Foreign Relations, Flipper waged an unsuccessful battle to over-turn his dishonorable discharge. He was still fighting when he died in Atlanta in 1940.

Thirty-five years after Flipper's death, his niece, Irsle King, and Ray MacColl, a teacher at Valdosta State University, marshaled forces that petitioned the Army Board for Correction of Military Records on Flipper's behalf. In December 1976 the board acknowledged that the military had committed a gross, racially motivated injustice and granted Flipper a posthumous honorable discharge and restored his second lieutenant's rank. Two years later Flipper's remains were returned from Atlanta and buried with full military honors beside his parents at Thomasville's Old Magnolia Cemetery. That same year, a Thomasville branch post office was named the Lt. Henry Ossian Flipper Substation. In 1999 President Clinton issued a presidential pardon, observing that, "this good man has now completely recovered his good name. Although the wheels of justice turn slowly at times, still they do turn."

Henry Ossian Flipper's star-crossed life ended at his gravesite in Thomasville's Old Magnolia Cemetery. Born a slave, Flipper graduated from West Point, was unjustly dishonorably discharged from the army, and received a presidential pardon in 1999, fifty-nine years after his death.

West Point responded to his reinstatement by installing a bust of Flipper in the academy library and creating the annual Henry O. Flipper Award to the graduating cadet who "Best typified the attributes of Flipper—leadership, self-discipline, and perseverance in the face of unusual difficulties while a cadet." The first award was presented in 1977 by Irsle King's grandson, Lt. William R. Davis, a U.S. Air Force Academy graduate.

A bust similar to the one at West Point is in the conference room (named for him) at Thomasville's main library. Henry O. Flipper Park is across the street from his grave site.

Thomasville is on U.S. Highway 19/319/84, 235 miles southeast of Atlanta and 35 miles north of Tallahassee, Florida. Flipper sites are open to the public. Self-guided tour booklets are available at the Thomasville Visitors Center, 401 South Broad Street. Phone (866) 577–3600. The Thomasville Black Heritage Trail guided tour is available by phone (229) 228–6983, and e-mail to Jack Hadley, jachadle@rose.net. It includes Flipper sites and other African-American landmarks.

Where There's Smoke . . .
Thomasville

C. W. Lapham wasn't about to get burned twice. The wealthy shoe manufacturer suffered severe lung damage during the Great Chicago Fire of 1871. So when he built his triwinged burgundy-and-mustard-colored Queen Anne Victorian mansion on Thomasville's Dawson Street in 1885, he made certain he'd always have an easy way out. All nineteen rooms have exits to the outside.

None of the rooms is symmetrical. Since there are no right angles in nature, he thought it prudent to build the house totally right-angle free. He could shudder at his near-death experience every time he looked at a cow's head design in the third-floor balcony woodwork, said to be an image of the bovine that legend says kicked over Mrs. O'Leary's lantern and started the fire that devastated the Windy City and turned poor C. W. into a lifelong pyrophobe. The entire third floor seems to be shaped like a fireman's helmet. Ironically, years after Lapham's death from pneumonia, his former wife, living on an Arizona cattle ranch, burned to death when a kerosene lamp she was carrying exploded and set her clothes on fire.

Lapham-Patterson State Historic Site is at 626 North Dawson Street, Thomasville. Admission fee. Call (229) 225–4004 or visit www.gastateparks.org.

Visitors needing a quick exit from the Lapham-Patterson House don't have far to go. When Chicago shoe manufacturer C. W. Lapham built his Thomasville home in 1885, he included outside exits in all nineteen rooms. He'd been injured in the Chicago fire of 1871 and wasn't about to let it happen again.

LAPHAM-PATTERSON HOUSE

Georgia Department of Natural Resources
Parks and Historic Sites Div

THOMASVILLE'S BIG OAK

The year is 1685 (or thereabouts). The Georgia Crown Colony is not even a gleam in his English Majesty's eye. Bands of Creeks and other Native Americans lead their happy-go-lucky lives in what a century or so later will become the southwestern corner of the fourth state of a newfangled notion called the United States. Deep in the forest, unnoticed by the birds and squirrels, an acorn spawns a sprout, which through the Revolution, Civil War, and World Wars grows into a live oak tree (*Quercus virginiana*), an evergreen of extraordinary proportions. Spreading over the corner of Monroe and Crawford Streets in downtown Thomasville, the Big Oak stands 75 feet high with a girth of 24 feet. Limbs spanning 162 feet are strung together by cables, and every time a good stiff wind blows through town, nervous Thomasvillians run over to make sure the venerable old fella is still holding his own.

Big Pig Jig
Vienna

My, oh, my, how this little piggy has grown. The Big Pig Jig was launched in 1982 when some Dooly County gourmets made wagers on who could cook the most succulent pig. They decided to settle the issue with a barbecue cooking competition linked with the county livestock association's annual hog show. Twenty cooking teams competed for $1,000 in prize money. Lured by the seductive aromas, several thousand salivating people showed up, sampled the 'cue, salivated some more, and demanded that the contest go on the next year. And so it has. Today the Big Pig Jig is big stuff—"Georgia's Official Barbecue Cooking Contest." The second weekend of October, 25,000 spectators come to the festival grounds on I-75 at Vienna (VIGH-enna) to admire the craftsmanship of 115 teams cooking more than 300 entries of whole hogs, shoulders, and ribs and kettles of sauce and Brunswick stew. It's judged by 425 experts who award several thousand dollars in prize money, trophies, blue ribbons, bragging rights, and the honor of representing the state of Georgia at the annual Pig Cook-off in Memphis—the World Series and Super Bowl of the barbecuing arts. If you ask the winning teams the secrets of their successful sauce and Brunswick stew, they'll likely say, with only half a smile: "I could tell you, but then I'd have to kill you."

If you'd like to be on hand, call the Dooly County Chamber of Commerce at (229) 268–8275 or visit www.doolychamber.com or www .bigpigjig.com. Vienna is off I-75 exit 109, 60 miles south of Macon.

This sign welcomes visitors to West Point Lake.

Baby, Give Me Some Grits

Warwick

In 1997 folks in the tiny Worth County town of Warwick—population 430—decided they needed a big-time festival to officially welcome spring to their corner of southwest Georgia. They wanted to name their festival for something everybody liked, but cherry blossoms, dogwoods, sorghum, onions, peaches, pigs, pecans, peanuts (the town's mainstay), gnats, buzzards, rattlesnakes, mules, and crawfish were already spoken for. So they said, collectively of course, "Nobody doesn't like grits." It was a natural, so to speak, and the National Grits Festival was born. The first few mid-April festivals drew about 5,000 folks, which is pretty fair, considering all the competition from other festivals saluting various critters, vegetables, bugs, fruits, and flowers.

Then, lo and behold, the 2002 Georgia General Assembly twice-blessed Warwick. First the esteemed ladies and gentlemen passed legislation making grits "The Official Processed Food of Georgia." Then they declared Warwick the state's grits capital. In 2003, Georgia governor Sonny Perdue declared Warwick "The Grits Capital of the World." With its new "capital" status, attendance at the National Grits Festival has more than doubled, as grits fanciers rushed in from as far away as Atlanta (160 miles north), Albany and Cordele (17 and 15 miles north and south, respectively), and little towns across south Georgia and north Florida, where nothing much happens on Saturday anyhow. Around James Emerson Park—named for the town's police chief, killed in the line of duty in 1968—everybody rolled up their sleeves and got in the spirit of the antique tractor show, beauty pageant, arts and crafts, the corn shucking contest, grits cooking, and eating all kinds of dishes imaginative cooks concocted from their favorite food. Among the crowd-pleasers are Pineapple Grits Pie, Pizza Grits, Grits Peach Pie, Zucchini Potato Grits, and Jimmy Carter's Baked Cheese Grits. For the sweet tooth Earline Smith's Chocolate-covered Grits look like tens of thousands of bubbling bonbons. Yu-ummm. All recipes are compiled in the popular festival cookbook.

The big event of the day is the group wallow in the Grits Pit. Contestants weigh in before they plunge into a cattle trough filled to the brim with cold cooked Quaker Instant Grits. First prize goes to the wallower who comes out of the trough with the greatest quantity of grits stuck to him/herself and his/her clothing. The losers have to figure a way to get the ooey-gooey Southern porridge out of their clothes, hair, and various orifices. A high-pressure fire hose seems to work best. Once cleaned up, everybody joins the big street party and dance and starts looking forward to next year's soiree.

No festival is worth its butter, salt, and pepper without an official fight song. Five-year-old Warwicker Michael McDaniel wrote this rousing tribute to his favorite dish:

I'm from Warwick, Georgia, and I know what I want to eat,
I don't want no oatmeal, and I don't want no cream of wheat,
Give me some grits, baby, give me some grits,
You can eat it with cheese, you can eat it with butter,
You can eat it anytime, with anything you please,
As long as it's grits, baby, just give me some grits,
Warwick, Georgia, grits capital of the world.

Warwick is on Highway 300, 12 miles west of I–75 exit 99. If you don't want to miss out on the fun, phone the Grits Hotline at (229) 881–6297 or visit www.gritsfest.com.

GRITS IS GROCERIES

In 2002 grits became the newest member of the symbol family, when the General Assembly ordained it as "the Official Processed Food of the State of Georgia." Under House Bill 993 so designating it, the lawmakers found and determined the following:

1) "Grits are bits of ground corn and hominy which constitute a uniquely indigenous Southern food first produced by Native Americans centuries ago; and

2) "Grammatically, the word 'grits' enjoys the notable distinction of being a rare noun which may be properly used as either singular or plural in writing and speaking; and

3) "According to the October 1999 issue of *Smithsonian* magazine, it can be argued that grits are America's first food, as evidenced by the Powhatan Indians' serving of cracked maize porridge to the country's first European settlers; and

4) "This prepared food is well known to all Georgians, but may initially be a source of confusion to visitors who've been told they grow on grits trees; and

5) "The preparation of grits has been praised through countless recipes and many literary endeavors and cookbooks; and

6) "It has been said of grits with literal truth that no one can eat just one."

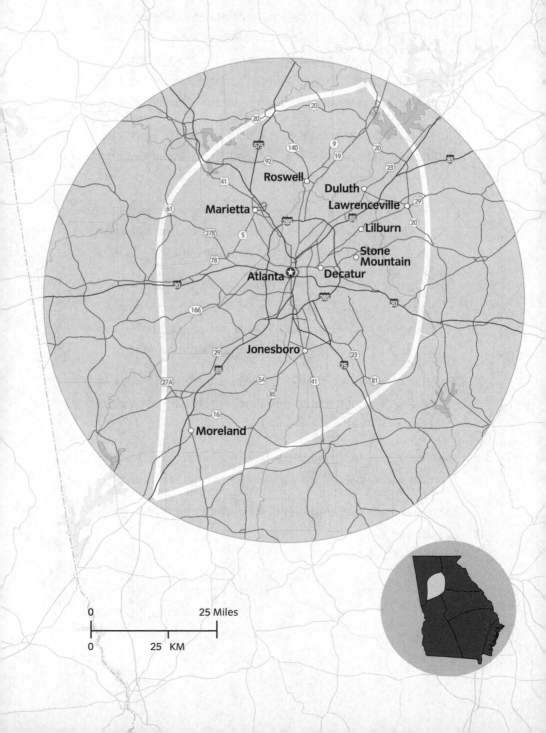

METRO ATLANTA

Roswell
Duluth
Lawrenceville
Marietta
Lilburn
Stone
Mountain
Atlanta
Decatur
Jonesboro
Moreland

0   25 Miles

0   25 KM

METRO ATLANTA

Half of all Georgians (4.5 million of us, and counting way too fast) live in Metro Atlanta's maze of cities, suburbs, and small towns on the verge of becoming cities and suburbs. Among malls and hair-pulling traffic that march relentlessly from near the Blue Ridge foothills nearly to Alabama, you can gawk at the Big Chicken and search for Dear Peggy, fairy shrimp, the two-headed snake, and Buster the Dearly Departed Police Dog. The Politically Correct Police may disparage it, but *Gone With the Wind* is still revered. Lovers of the 1936 novel and 1939 movie come from around the world to visit the author's apartment in Atlanta's Margaret Mitchell House and Museum, the Road to Tara Museum in Jonesboro, and "Miss Peggy's" grave in Oakland Cemetery. Like the romanticized Old South, genuine Southern accents are also mostly gone with the wind. You're much more likely to hear voices from New York and New England, California, Mexico, Cuba, Korea, and Vietnam. For insights into Atlanta's multiple personalities, read the collected wisdom of Lewis Grizzard and novels by erstwhile Atlantan Anne Rivers Siddons.

The Two-Faced Snake
Atlanta

Cynics would say that the two-faced snake in the Georgia Capitol Museum is right at home in the building where the legislature does its business every year. They suspect there might be some collusion between the little midlands water snake and the esteemed ladies and gentlemen, because the snake escaped a purge that removed a photo of stuffed poker-playing squirrels from the fourth-floor exhibit. Not to worry, the glass cases still hold a gracious wealth of exhibits on cotton, peanuts, and peaches and mounted birds, deer, raccoons, possums, bugs, bears, wildcats, fish, flora and fauna, rocks and minerals, Native American artifacts, historical what-nots, tattered Civil War flags, and paintings and marble busts of bygone statesmen. (Seeing the noble images of men who were worthy and others who were rascals, I'm reminded of what Bette Davis said on the death of archrival Joan Crawford: "Just because a person's dead, doesn't mean she's changed.") Georgia's sort-of copy of the U.S. Capitol was completed in 1889—twenty-one years after uppity carpetbag Atlanta succeeded Milledgeville as the state's capital city. In 1956 the 75-foot-high dome was crowned with 43 ounces of 23-karat gold picked out of the northeast Georgia hills around Dahlonega. Whenever the gilding starts getting tatty, the good folks up that way sing, "Hi-ho, hi-ho, it's off to work we go," and come down with another wagonload. The building is open for guided and self-guided tours Monday through Friday. From January to March you can sit in the House and Senate galleries and watch the legislative wheels grind ever so agonizingly slowly. Caveat emptor: Aristotle or some other very wise man once said, "Sausages and laws are two things you don't want to watch being made."

The capitol is hard to miss. It's the Greek temple–looking affair with Corinthian columns, an outside statuary garden, and a big glitzy hard hat on the southside of downtown Atlanta at Washington Street and Capitol Avenue, across from Atlanta's City Hall. Phone (404) 656–2844.

A Hanging in Midtown

Atlanta

Midtown Atlanta's high-rise condos, snazzy eateries, and bars seem an unlikely locale for a hanging. But on June 7, 1862, Confederate authorities hanged James J. Andrews as a Union spy for masterminding "The Great Locomotive Chase." An historical marker at Juniper and Third streets marks the spot where the gallows stood in what was then a rural area, far from the city center. On June 18, seven other "Andrews Raiders" were hanged together in southeast Atlanta.

Their saga began on April 12, 1862, when Andrews and twenty disguised Union soldiers boarded a northbound train at Marietta. While the train's crew was breakfasting in a trackside hotel at Big Shanty (Kennesaw), Andrews Raiders train-jacked the locomotive *General* and three box cars. They planned to cut telegraph lines and rails and burn bridges the l00 miles from Big Shanty to Chattanooga. They were foiled by Confederate Capt. William Fuller, the *General*'s conductor. Shouting, "Someone who has no right to has gone off with our train!" Fuller and fellow crewmen chased the pirated engine on foot, by handcar, and in the commandeered locomotive *Texas* and captured Andrews and his raiders, at Ringgold, 87 miles from the scene of the crime.

Andrews and seven others were condemned to death and brought to Atlanta for hanging, ironically on a train pulled by *General*. The eight are buried side by side, with a memorial to their heroism, in Chattanooga's National Cemetery. Seven were posthumously awarded the first Congressional Medal of Honor. A civilian scout and spy employed by the Union Army, Andrews was not eligible for the military medal. Heroes are in the eye of the beholder, and Capt. William Fuller, who died in 1905, rests with honor in Atlanta's historic Oakland Cemetery. "The Great Locomotive Chase" was dramatized in the 1955 Walt Disney film, with Fess Parker of 1950s TV *Davy Crockett* fame as Andrews. The *General* has an honored place in the Southern Museum of Civil War and Locomotive History in Kennesaw. The *Texas* is in the Cyclorama building in Atlanta's Grant Park.

Super Salmon
Atlanta

Atlanta's flossy Buckhead entertainment district couldn't stand to let the burbs have the honor of the biggest, baddest critter in the metro area. So in the mid-1990s, the Atlanta Fish Market, a popular seafood restaurant, stationed a 65-foot copper-clad spawning salmon, leaping above rivers of traffic at 265 Pharr Road in the heart of the party-hearty district. About the only thing bigger in Buckhead is the collective "morning after" shared by the weekend's dedicated partyers. Call (404) 262–3165.

TAKE TWO ASPIRIN AND RENEW YOUR PASSPORT

Sign on a medical laboratory:

PREGNANCY TEST, AIDS TESTING, VENEREAL DISEASE TREATMENTS, PREMARITAL BLOOD TESTING, DRUG SCREENING, VIAGRA, IMMIGRATION PHYSICALS, PASSPORT PHOTOS.

If your test doesn't turn out the way you hoped, your passport may be your best option.

Gone with Miss Peggy
Atlanta

Margaret Mitchell's motto might've been, "Don't wish for something, because, sweetpea, you might sure enough get it." Affectionately known as "Atlanta's dear Peggy," Miss Mitchell devoted much of her adult life to creating a little Civil War tale she called *Gone With the Wind*. To her amazement, it sold millions of copies in every known language and was made into a film people around the world still weep over. Horrified by the glare, she became the Emily Dickinson of Southern literature, went into seclusion, and swore off further literary ventures.

When she died in 1949—struck by a taxi on her beloved Peachtree Street—Peggy sought the serenity of a simple tombstone in downtown Atlanta's historic Oakland Cemetery: "Margaret Mitchell Marsh. Born Atlanta, Ga., Nov. 8, 1900. Died Atlanta, Ga., Aug. 16, 1949." It's planted with roses, her favorite flower.

If she ever decides to dust off her battered old Remington portable in the afterlife, she'll have fodder for many a ripping yarn. Her 100,000 "neighbors" in Oakland's eighty-eight park-like acres go back to 1850, when the cemetery received its first guests. They include Moses Formwalt, the city's first mayor, in the 1840s, and Maynard H. Jackson, Jr., the first African-American mayor, whose resting place views the downtown skyline, which grew dramatically under his three 1970s terms. Four Georgia governors can pine for their glory days under the State Capitol's gold dome, winking seductively on the horizon.

Grand Slammer Robert Tyre "Bobby" Jones probably wishes he could chip a few shots around Oakland's grassy lawns. Many fans leave golf balls on his grave in his honor, and for luck with their own game. He's been out of the loop since 1971 and would no doubt appreciate a new set of clubs.

Within the old redbrick walls are wealthy merchants in house-size Victorian, Greek Revival, and Egyptian Revival mausoleums, with stained-glass windows and wrought-iron benches; and 17,000

Admirers of "Grand Slam" golf legend Bobby Jones leave something he can putt and chip with on his grave in Atlanta's historic Oakland Cemetery. Now, if only they'd leave him a new set of clubs, he could probably get up an after-hours foursome.

nameless paupers in a Potters Field; Jewish and African-American sections; saints, characters, and rascals. The recumbent "Lion of Atlanta," a replica of Switzerland's "Lion of Lucerne," resting on a Confederate battle flag, guards the graves of 6,900 Confederate soldiers and sixteen Union soldiers, who died in Atlanta hospitals. "Tweet the Mockingbird" is one of several pets interred near their owners.

Oakland Cemetery is at 248 Oakland Avenue, near downtown Atlanta. Open daylight hours daily. Free admission. The visitor center in the 1899 Bell Tower Building has self-guided maps, books, and restrooms. Guided tours are led on weekends. Phone (404) 688–2107. After you've visited the spirits, step across the street for lively spirits, oyster po' boys, and fried catfish and calamari tacos, "served by happy, warm-hearted souls" at Six Feet Under Pub & Fish House, 415 Memorial Drive, (404) 523–6644.

Gone with the Wind author Margaret Mitchell was publicity-shy, even after death. *GWTW* pilgrims hunting for her whereabouts will find her, beside her husband, John Marsh, in this unostentatious gravesite in downtown Atlanta's historic Oakland Cemetery.

MARGARET MITCHELL MARSH
BORN ATLANTA, GA.
NOV. 8, 1900
DIED ATLANTA, GA.
AUG. 16, 1949

MARSH

JOHN ROBERT MARSH
BORN MAYSVILLE
OCT. 6, 18
DIED ATLAN
MAY 5

Sister Melanie and Doc Holliday
Atlanta

Margaret Mitchell based her fictional married cousins Melanie Hamilton and Ashley Wilkes on a frustrated love affair between her real-life third cousin Mattie Holliday and famous Western gunslinger John Henry "Doc" Holliday. Born in Griffin, Georgia, on August 14, 1851, Holliday studied dentistry in Philadelphia and set up practice in Atlanta, where he fell in love with his sixteen-year-old first cousin Mattie, a cousin of Margaret Mitchell's mother. When the Catholic Church denied the cousins permission to marry, Mattie joined a convent in Savannah and took the name Sister Mary Melanie. When she was assigned to Atlanta's St. Joseph Infirmary in the 1920s, she and Margaret Mitchell became close friends. She gave Margaret permission to use her convent name, Melanie, in her book, as long as the character was "somebody nice." Prevented from marrying Mattie, "Doc" Holliday went West, where he achieved immortality with Wyatt Earp in the gunfight at the OK Corral. He and Sister Melanie corresponded until his death in Colorado in 1887. Long, lanky, blond Holliday was purportedly Margaret's inspiration for Southern gentleman Ashley Wilkes. She obligingly "married" him to Melanie in the pages of *Gone With the Wind*.

The Margaret Mitchell House and *Gone With the Wind* Museum is at 999 Peachtree Street; (404) 249–7015. Admission fee.

What It Is, Is . . . Art

Atlanta

When it was dedicated in 1999, an Atlanta critic said it was the ugliest excuse for art he'd ever seen. Passersby think it's a building being demolished, or a new one under construction.

Beauty, as they say, is in the eye of the beholder, and those who see beauty in *54 Columns* have "eyes" the majority apparently don't possess. It's a collection of fifty-four bare cinderblock columns, ranging in height from 10 to 20 feet, arranged on a triangular lot at the corner of Highland Avenue and Glen Iris Drive, in Atlanta's regentrifying Old Fourth Ward neighborhood.

Connecticut artist Sol Lewitt, internationally renowned for his minimalist concrete creations, says *54 Columns* represents the urban environment through repeated lines and geometric forms. The columns are intended to echo Atlanta's downtown skyline, which peeks above the trees on the sculpture's west side. The work was a gift to the city by Atlanta art patrons, the High Museum of Art ,and the Fulton County Arts Council's Public Art Program.

Love it or hate it, *54 Columns*, with its cinderblock stalagmites, is hard to ignore.

105

While some critics scorn it, the prestigious arts journal *Art In America* included *54 Columns* among its top twenty-four public arts projects in 2000. Some of Lewitt's less cumbersome pieces are in New York's Museum of Modern Art, London's Tate Gallery, and Atlanta's High Museum of Art. Another of his massive concrete pieces, *Tower with Vertical Blocks 1*, is on the Emory University campus, a few miles from *54 Columns*.

The Bridge
Atlanta

Bikers and joggers on the paved Freedom Trail, which passes *54 Columns* on its way through Freedom Park, can ponder another piece of what-is-it? art. At first sight, *The Bridge,* at Ponce de Leon Avenue and Freedom Parkway, resembles a haphazard heap of scrap metal, with a mule, junked cars, old tires, and other discards poking from the elongated pile. Created by Alabama artist Thornton Dial and dedicated in September, 2005, it's a tribute to Civil Rights icon John Lewis, now a U.S. Congressman from Atlanta.

Looking east on Ponce de Leon Avenue, an abstract mule, wheat, and a tractor on the left side of the sculpture symbolize Lewis's early life in rural Alabama. Then figures cross a bridge, symbolizing his transition to urban life and his role in the 1960s Civil Rights movement, highlighted by his participation in a voting rights march over Selma, Alabama's Edmund Pettus Bridge on Bloody Sunday, March 7, 1965. Assaulted by truncheon-wielding Alabama state troopers, Lewis and dozens of other marchers were severely beaten. Protected by national troops, Lewis led another march over the bridge, the first leg of the historic Selma-to-Montgomery March, which led to passage of the Voting Rights Act.

The Bridge, on Atlanta's Ponce de Leon Avenue, symbolizes the long, often hazardous climb of civil rights icon John Lewis, now the district's U.S. representative.

Dude, Can You Spare . . .

Atlanta

Where have all the hippies gone? Dude, they've gone to Little Five Points. Graying hipsters, orange-haired young hips, bikers, Goth punks, long hairs, skinheads, braided Rastas, dropouts, inconoclasts and counterculturists, Ward and June, and the Bradys in for a peek of life beyond the Suburban Curtain blend in a psychedelic stew around the junction of Moreland and Euclid Avenues, three miles northeast of downtown Atlanta.

They hang around their Southern-fried Haight-Asbury throwback, beat bongos and read poetry for handouts, and maneuver skateboards and roller blades through the crowded sidewalks. They get tattooed, Mohawked and shaved, body parts pierced, hair tinted peach and magenta. The Junkman's Daughter and Stefan's outfit them in cammos, leather and chains, knees-out denims, tie-dye, grunge, and 10-league boots with truck tire soles, cool T-shirts,

Dude, can you spare some change for some funky threads and other cool stuff at The Junkman's Daughter in Atlanta's Little Five Points neighborhood?

molting boas, mothy mink stoles, and '60s prom dresses fit for a queen (or a drag queen). They go deliriously deaf on heavy metal at The Point; worship at Community Bar's Elvis shrine; dine on enchiladas, curry, tofu burgers, pizza, tofu, and organic broccoli; star in yeasty street theater; and remain ever vigilant for corporate interlopers like Starbucks, which crashed the pad in 1999.

Dude, can you spare a dime?

What'll Ya Have?
Atlanta

It doesn't commemorate a stirring battle, a hero or heroine, or the glory of the city's 1996 Summer Olympics. But to many Atlantans, The Varsity Drive-In is as noble as any stone or bronze memorial. Opened in 1928 by Georgia Tech dropout Frank Gordy, and still owned by his descendants, The Varsity has evolved from a simple snack shack, quelling the hunger of Tech students, into what is purportedly the world's largest drive-in restaurant.

A trip to The Varsity is a rite of passage for dating teenagers, and site of many proposals, marriages, and anniversaries. Thousands of others need no excuse but a craving for good, simple American eats to show up daily to demolish two miles of grilled hot dogs, topped with 300 gallons of chili, frosted orange shakes, burgers, fried pies, and deliciously greasy fried onion rings and french fries in vast, covered parking areas, with space for 630 cars served by an army of car waiters, and in five indoor dining rooms with 800 school-desk seats and TVs tuned to sports, sit-coms, and soap operas.

Late comedian Nipsey Russell, who died in 2005, began his career carrying trays and entertaining Varsity patrons. Old-timers also remember John "Flossie Mae" Raiford, a jive-talking pre-hip-hopper famous for

his outrageous outfits and outlandish hats, with rotary phones, cans of Raid, and other accessories balanced precariously on top. After fifty-six years, Flossie Mae toted his last trays in 1993. He was eighty-six.

Former Atlantans back for a visit put a Varsity "grease fix" at the top of their "must-do" list.

Behind the 150-foot-long serving bar, dozens of counterfolk in red-and-white soda-fountain style paper hats, chant, "What'll ya have?" to the hungry hordes, who respond, "Two glorified steaks" (hamburger with mayo, lettuce, and tomato); "a naked dog walking" (plain hot dog to go); "a yellow dog" (hot dog with mustard); "a bird" (grilled chicken sandwich); "a bag of rags" (potato chips); "strings and rings" (French fries and onion rings); and "FO" (orange shake so thick it requires a spoon).

Over the years the guest list has included Clark Gable, Bob Hope, Joe Montana, Jimmy Buffett, Franklin D. Roosevelt, George H. W. Bush, Bill Clinton, and Jimmy and Rosalynn Carter (numerous times). Elvis ordered cheeseburgers "walking" whenever he was in town. *The Today Show*'s Katie Couric stood behind the counter and shouted "What'll ya have?" to amazed patrons during Atlanta's 1996 Summer Olympics.

Many chili impresarios guard their "secret sauce" like a family heirloom. For instance, if you ask chefs at Vienna's Big Pig Jig for their recipes, they'll grit their teeth and say, "I could tellya, but then I'd havta killya." The Varsity happily puts its sauce recipe on its Web site.

The Varsity is at Spring Street and North Avenue and Interstate 75/85, near Georgia Tech, on downtown Atlanta's northern edge. Phone (404) 881–1706; Web site www.thevarsity.com. Five other Varsitys are in Metro Atlanta and Athens, but true believers say the best grease fix is the original.

"What'll ya have?" Sharyn Smith is inhaling a Varsity chili dog, with a supporting cast of fried onion rings and a frosted orange, topped off by a fried peach pie a la mode. In Atlanta, the Varsity is at the top of the fast-food pyramid.

VARSITY CHILI SAUCE

When you are topping a hot dog or hamburger with chili sauce, it is vital that the consistency be uniform, no meat chunks allowed. This method is traditional among the nation's hot dog chefs and they are avid about the beef having to be nearly pulverized. If you cannot grind your own, see if you can have a butcher make an extra-fine grind for this recipe, which makes enough to top six hot dogs:

2 garlic cloves, minced
½ cup onions, chopped fine
2 tablespoons vegetable oil
1 pound lean ground beef
1 teaspoon salt
½ teaspoon ground black pepper
1 tablespoon yellow mustard
1 tablespoon vinegar
1 teaspoon Worcestershire sauce
½ teaspoon Tabasco, or to taste
¼ cup ketchup
½ to 1 cup tomato juice

In a large heavy skillet, cook garlic and onion over moderate heat, stirring until onion is softened. Add beef and cook, stirring and breaking up any lumps with a fork, until cooked through. Drain off any excess fat, if desired. Add remaining ingredients, adding just enough juice to create a very loose but not soupy mixture, stirring occasionally, about ten minutes.

Historic Decatur Cemetery
Decatur

A stainless-steel bench shaped like an armless reclining man seems to be saying, "Come sit a spell; remember those who rest here." Located near historic Decatur Cemetery's Bell Street entrance, the bench marks no grave. It was placed in a grassy plot by the family of an eighteen-year-old Eagle Scout (1979–97) buried nearby. All are welcome to rest in the figure's comfortable lap.

Metro Atlanta's oldest public burial grounds, the cemetery predates Decatur's 1823 incorporation, making it more than a decade older than Atlanta's Oakland Cemetery (see "Gone with Miss Peggy"). Among the most senior residents are Revolutionary War, Civil War, and War of 1812 veterans; early 1800s settlers under rough, lichen-crusted stones; and members of the Candler family (Coca-Cola) and others whose names appear on local streets, public buildings, schools, parks, and hospitals.

How thoughtful of an Eagle Scout's family to put this comfy stainless steel bench by his grave in Decatur Cemetery. When you've rested, you can trek around the graves of early 1800s pioneers and Revolutionary War, Civil War, and War of 1812 casualties.

Entrances are on Bell Street (off Church Street, two blocks from the courthouse square), and Commerce Drive in downtown Decatur. If you would like to see it, take the MARTA (Metropolitan Atlanta Rapid Transit Authority) train to Decatur Station and walk ten minutes. Open daily. Call (404) 378–4411.

Luthers: Ultimate Hamdogs and Fried Twinkies

Decatur

Maybe you were watching *The Tonight Show with Jay Leno* on June 8, 2005, and were (a) horrified, (b) driven to manic hunger, (c) a combination of both, by a gastronomic artery bomb prepared by Chandler Goff, proprietor of Mulligans Bar, in Decatur's Oakhurst neighborhood. With Wolfgang Puck aplomb, Goff shaped a half-pound hamburger patty and halved a sugar-glazed Krispy-Kreme doughnut and laid them on a grease-popping grill, meanwhile deep-frying slices of bacon. When the burger was sizzled to his liking, he topped it with a slice of American cheese and the bacon and placed it between the warm doughnut "buns." Leno, the show's crew, and guests grinned in childlike ecstasy as the burgers' juices dripped down their chins.

"We call it The Luther Burger in homage to [late R&B crooner] Luther Vandross," explains Goff, a Birmingham, Alabama, native and graduate of Atlanta's Emory University, who sold investments for eight years before a friend talked him into co-owning a bar.

"Then he left for New York, and I got stuck with it," he laughs.

That was in 2001; then, along came The Luther.

"One of our cooks brought in a copy of *Rolling Stone* with an article about Vandross. He was skinny then and was reflecting on his heavier days. He said he woke up hungry in the middle of the night and started to make a hamburger, but he didn't have any buns, so he used doughnuts and it became a favorite snack of his. We figured we'd do it here, really as kind of a joke. In Birmingham, my mother used to cut Krispy-Kremes in half and toast them. I liked that pretty well, so we tried it here among ourselves and it was delicious. We put it on the menu and it sells really well, especially late at night when we have live music."

The Luther made *The Tonight Show* when an Atlanta newspaper story picked up by the Associated Press caught Jay Leno's interest.

"One of Leno's producers called and said, 'Jay really wants to try it. He loves junk food and hasn't eaten a vegetable in five years. He'll eat an entire large pizza in one sitting. The only way he'll shut up about this thing is for us to fly you out to the show.' So I went out to LA and it was a great experience. I cooked Luthers for Jay and the crew and the Tony Keith Band that was on the show that night. They ate a ton of 'em."

Leave carb and calorie cares at the front door when you overload on a Luther Burger at Mulligans Bar in Decatur's Oakhurst neighborhood. Be sure to save room for a Fried Twinkie.

Add a side of fries, chili, slaw, or potato salad and you've got a banquet on a bun tipping the scales at about 750–850 calories. Not to mention "your favorite beverage" to ease it down.

Like many greenhorns, I approached The Luther with fear and trepidation. Hamburger on a Krispy-Kreme? You're kidding, right? But after the first timid bite, I wolfed it all down and licked the plate. As Goff says, it's similar to sopping sausage in pancake syrup, and grilling takes away some of the doughnut's sweetness.

The "Creations" section of Mulligans' menu has other gastronomic delights. The off-the-calories-chart Ultimate Hamdog is a hot dog wrapped in a hamburger patty, fried and served on a hoagie roll with chili, bacon, a fried egg, and French fries on top. After courting calories/cholesterol hari-kari, you might as well go all the way with a Fried Twinkie—a pair of Twinkies egg-washed, wrapped in pulverized Cap'n Crunch Cereal, deep-fried, and topped with chocolate and cherry sauce. Yu-umm.

Mindful of their patrons' well-being, Mulligans' menu has a caveat: "We here at Mulligans hope you have the sense to realize that, although delicious, we do not recommend eating fried foods every day and remind you to exercise regularly and get an annual physical."

Caveat No. 2 (not on the menu): Luther Vandross never fully recovered from a debilitating stroke he suffered in April, 2003. He died on July 1, 2005, less than a month after his "inspiration" was featured on Jay Leno. He was fifty-four.

Mulligans serves Luthers, Ultimate Hamdogs, Fried Twinkies, and other less intimidating fare every day at 630 East Lake Drive, Decatur. Phone (404) 377–0108 or visit www.thehamdog.com.

Sentimental Journey: Southeastern Railway Museum
Duluth

Long ago travelers used to lament, "Whether I'm going to heaven or hell, I know I'll have to change trains in Atlanta." With the demise of passenger trains, that baton has been passed to Atlanta's busiest-on-earth international airport. Those who'd like to relive those thrilling days of yesteryear—when we rode in comfort and style on *The Twentieth-century Limited, The Royal Palm, Super Chief,* and other luxury liners on wheels—can come on out to the Southeastern Railway Museum in Duluth, 20 miles northeast of downtown Atlanta. Owned and operated by the Atlanta chapter of the Southeastern Railway Historical Society, the thirty-acre indoor and outdoor museum invites us to find a seat in red cabooses, hauled around the yards by full-sized diesel locomotives. On the third Saturday of every month, cabooses are hitched to huffing, puffing vintage steam locomotives ("Chattanooga Choo Choo, Won't You Choo-Choo Me Home?"). Before and after the ride, there's lots of time to get a close-up look at more than ninety pieces of rolling stock, exhibits, and displays on the golden age of passenger trains, which started accelerating downhill about the time Harry Truman's 1948 "Whistle Stop" campaign blew Tom Dewey's political aspirations into the ash can.

One of the stars is *Superb*, the 1911 Pullman car that hauled President Warren G. Harding across the country on official and unofficial business in the early 1920s. (Speak, you walls!) After Harding's mysterious death in San Francisco in 1923 (his wife was suspected of poisoning the playboy prez in retaliation for his flagrant contretemps with a much younger woman), *Superb* hailed the chief back to Washington and thence to burial in his hometown of Marion, Ohio. World War II army chefs prepared SOS and other delicacies for troops in a military kitchen car parked nearby. You can walk through locomotives, passenger coaches, dining cars, a railway post office car, and Pullman sleeper cars ("Please refrain while the train is standing in the station"). Kids and grown-up "kids" who enjoy model railroading can see the miniature train go round and round in the museum's exhibit hall.

From downtown Atlanta take Interstate 85 north to exit 104/Pleasant Hill Road and follow the signs. Phone (770) 476–2013 or visit www.srm duluth.org. A fee is charged, but rides are unlimited. All aboard!

Shell Annie
Jonesboro

Peter Bonner, raconteur and guide with Historical & Hysterical Tours, offers this little-known vignette from the Civil War skirmishes around Jonesboro, south of Atlanta: "During the fighting around Jonesboro, on August 31, 1864, Union General John 'Blackjack' Logan's artillery fired a cannonball that went through the headboard of a pregnant lady's bed. It landed in a fireplace, but it was a solid shot, kind of like a bowling ball, and didn't explode. Well, the lady's father, the future baby's grand-father, ran out of the house, waving a sheet at the Union artillery. They sent a rider down to find out why this man was waving a sheet at them. He told them he wasn't trying to get involved in the fighting, but a baby was upstairs getting ready to be born, and the army needed to move their artillery to the right or left a few yards. Well, they were the enemy, but they were still Americans, so they obligingly moved the artillery away from the house. General Logan came down to the house with a cavalry detachment and brought a Catholic priest and medical officer, who went up and delivered the baby. The priest and medical officer were allowed to name the child—they named her, in Latin, 'Shellanna-marvellier,' which they said means "Marvelous escape from a shell." She was called Shell Annie for the rest of her life. A newspaper article from the time of the 1939 *Gone With the Wind* premiere in Atlanta verified the story and quoted her as saying she wished she'd been called Marvellier instead of Shell Annie. It sounded more ladylike."

As a side note Bonner says that Blackjack Logan financed the Cyclorama, the circumferential painting of the Battle of Atlanta that's exhibited in Atlanta's Grant Park, to foster his postwar political career in Illinois. It worked; he was elected to the U.S. Senate and was the Republican vice presidential candidate with James Blaine in 1884. They lost to Democrat Grover Cleveland. He's depicted in the painting, galloping bravely into battle on a black horse. If you'd like to hear Peter Bonner's war stories in person, contact him at (770) 477–8864; www.peterbonner.com.

ELVIS RIDES AGAIN

It couldn't be him, could it? Sure as shootin' looks like him. Yep, the Confederate flag bearer in a *Gone With the Wind* mural at the Road to Tara Museum in the Jonesboro Depot Welcome Center is "him," Elvis, the King himself. The painting was done by Atlanta artist Del Nichols, who finds a part for Elvis in everything he does. The museum has all kinds of other great *GWTW* stuff; 104 North Main Street, Jonesboro; (770) 478–4800 or (800) 662–7829; www.visitscarlett.com. Take I–75 exit 228/Stockbridge, turn right onto Highway 138, and go 5 miles to the depot. Admission fee.

Buster R.I.P.
Jonesboro

"Not just a dog, but a police officer, a partner, one who made a difference," reads the inscription on the grave of Buster, a five-year-old Clayton County Police dog who was killed in the line of duty. Fellow officers put up the granite monument with his image in front of police headquarters at 7930 North McDonough Street in Jonesboro after bad guys brought down the fearless crime fighter in 1990.

What a good dog. When Buster, a five-year-old crime fighter, was killed in the line of duty, members of the Clayton County Police Department put up this granite marker in his honor.

Drive-By Funeral
Jonesboro

An elegant horse-drawn hearse in Pope Dickson Funeral Home's Antique Funeral Museum led a cloak-and-dagger double life. In 1883 the hearse and matched pair of black horses bore the body of Georgia governor and former Confederate vice president Alexander Hamilton Stephens to his final resting place at Crawfordville, 70 miles east of Atlanta. "Little Alex" would no doubt have danced a fandango in his coffin had he known that during The Late Unpleasantness this same hearse smuggled runaway slaves to freedom. The smugglee would "play dead" in the bottom of a casket with a secret trapdoor. When the funeral procession crossed into a free Northern state, the "deceased" would slide open the trapdoor and shout "Hallelujah!" Confederate soldiers caught behind enemy lines used the bottomless hearse for a ride home.

The hearse is one of many pieces of Victorian funerary collected by the late Pope Dickson and his son, Abb Dickson, at what may be the world's only drive-by funeral museum. You can stay in your vehicle and get a passing look as you drive by, or park your rig in the lot behind the funeral home in downtown Jonesboro and come up to the big lighted windows for a closer examination. Among the other curiosities is a cast-iron "mummy case." Made by a Cincinnati company that also made wood stoves and skillets, the sealed casket's unique feature was an oval glass viewing plate that allowed mourners to see the dear departed's face without encountering discomfiting odors.

Sentimental Victorians wore two types of mourning jewelry; both types are on display here. A memorial ribbon and locket held a likeness of the deceased, and an "In Memory Of" pin had a lock of his/her hair. Mirrors in the home were turned to the wall, and pictures were draped in black. The departed was laid out for viewing on a "cooling board" and placed in the coffin only at the time of the funeral. Abb Dickson says that his collection preserves a unique era in history and pays tribute to the art of honoring someone after his or her death. "These are pieces of the past and a celebration of someone's life."

The Antique Funeral Museum is in the rear of Pope Dickson & Son Funeral Home, 168 McDonough Street, Jonesboro; (770) 478–7211. Follow the directions to the Depot Welcome Center above. The museum is a block over. The room isn't open, but the exhibits with written descriptions are lighted every night until 11:00 P.M.

Mary Frazier Long, Priviologist
Lawrenceville

Behind the house and barn it stood,
A hundred yards or more,
And hurrying feet a path had made,
Straight to its swinging door.
Its architecture was a form
Of simple classic art,
But in the tragedy of life
It played a major part.

—Author unknown

For a retired septuagenarian schoolteacher, Mary Frazier Long has an inordinate interest in bathroom humor. She gets phone calls from perfect strangers, sharing a few "toilet" jokes of their own. That's because Long has devoted more than two decades to assembling photos, stories, humor, historical facts, and trivia about outhouses.

"The first thing people tear down when they're moving up is the privy," she laments. "People don't want to get up in the middle of the night and run outside."

Mary Frazier Long's little book of privy-leged facts and poetry is now in its tenth edition. When you're traveling in off-the-beaten-path Georgia, it can be great reading and a real necessity.

In 1984, Long and her husband, Dean, published the first edition of *Old Georgia Privies*, a paperback with photos of outhouses in Georgia and elsewhere, spliced with poems and words of wisdom.

In 2004, the Longs published the tenth edition of *Old Georgia Privies*. The little softcover book (which sells for $10) is filled with sepia-toned photos of Peach State privies, as well as those of poet Carl Sandburg in Galesburg, Illinois; a Bosnian "ten-holer"; a two-door model at the Catacombs in Rome, Italy; an Irish outhouse in a cow pasture; and an English country "necessary."

Among the photos are poems and sayings by such notables as William Shakespeare, John Keats, Theodore Roosevelt, Eleanor Roosevelt, Adlai Stevenson, Voltaire, Mark Twain, Albert Einstein, St. Thomas Aquinas, and Winston Churchill. Most of it isn't privy-leged information, although Churchill does observe, "There is no time for ease and comfort. It is the time to dare and endure." Actor Glenn Ford notes, "If they try to rush me, I always say, I've got only one speed, and it's slower." Saith Thomas Alva Edison: "The best thinking has been done in solitude." From an anonymous source: "Life is like a roll of toilet tissue. The closer you get to the end, the faster it rolls out."

The Longs credit President Franklin Roosevelt with the proliferation of rural American privies. When FDR took office in 1933, he gave his Works Progress Administration (WPA) the task of providing "relief" for American farmers. Dubbed "Roosevelt Bungalows," more than 2.3 million of the slant-roofed, one-hole outies eventually dotted the countryside. Only a few still stand, most of them abandoned and forlorn.

The Longs frequently present a short course entitled "Privial Pursuit" (billed as a "Moving Experience") to organizations, community clubs, and church groups. Honorariums are given to a scholarship fund, and participants are awarded a "PhD" (Privy House Devotee).

If you'd like a copy of *Old Georgia Privies*, contact Mary Frazier Long, 288 Craig Drive, Lawrenceville. Phone (770) 962–6345.

This Old Seminary
Lawrenceville

A casual drive through Gwinnett County suggests that most everything in the northeast Metro Atlanta county was built not much earlier than a few months ago. A few structures in the county's older towns date from the early 1900s, when the county's population barely topped 10,000. Now a booming metropolis of 700,000 and growing fast, even those precious relics are on the threatened and endangered lists. Many are sacrificed with little fanfare for shiny, new shopping centers, schools, office parks, and housing developments.

But when executives of the Dairy Queen ice-cream chain eyed a broken-down little brick building on South Perry Street in downtown Lawrenceville, the county seat, alarms went off: Dairy Queen wants to tear down the Lawrenceville Female Seminary!

When the original 1838 seminary—a term for finishing schools that taught reading, writing, and social stratagems to antebellum young ladies—burned in 1850, the current two-story Greek Revival took its place. The bottom floor was devoted to education. The Lawrenceville Masonic lodge performed its rituals on the top floor.

Already a decade old, the Seminary survived Gen. William T. Sherman's sweep through Atlanta in 1864. It withstood the ripples of the Great Charleston, South Carolina, earthquake of 1886, and generations of rambunctious children. At various times, boys attended classes. It hosted Kiwanis, Lions Club, PTAs, garden clubs, and the United Daughters of the Confederacy, and for a time housed a radio station.

All of them took their toll, and by 1970 it seemed destined for a date with Dairy Queen. But up stepped Gwinnett County government, which purchased the building with a combination of state, federal, and local money. They had it placed on the National Register of Historic Places, safeguarding it in perpetuity from ice-cream vendors and others who'd defile it.

In 2005, the gussied up grande dame observed its sesquicentennial, marking 150 years.

The little building you could walk around in about three minutes now houses the Gwinnett History Museum's collection of farm implements, textiles, historic photos of Gwinnett, and exhibits on religion, schools, music, and other aspects of the county's life. Modern brides wanting a retro look can check out the old-timey wedding gown made of flour and cotton sacks. Call (770) 822–5178 or visit www.gwinnettparks.com.

Beau Knows

Lilburn

Folks up north depend on Pennsylvania's Punxsutawney Phil to prognosticate the coming of spring. At the Yellow River Game Ranch in Lilburn, hundreds show up before dawn on February 2 to see whether General Beauregard Lee has to say "yea" or "nay" about the season's imminent arrival. Beauregard takes his duties seriously. After all, in 2002 Governor Roy Barnes named Yellow River's resident groundhog "Georgia's Official Weather Prognosticator." So with the bundled-up crowd chanting "Go, Beau; go, Beau," a designated ringer clangs a big bell outside the General's cozy 4-foot-high white-brick knockoff of Tara. Beau's all toasty warm in there, and sometimes he takes a little coaxing. "When you only work but one day a year, sometimes it's hard to get yourself motivated," reasons Yellow River Ranch's CEO Art Rilling.

The crowd keeps chanting, and a few minutes after first light, Beau pokes his nose out the mansion door and waddles into the open. He looks around, doesn't see his shadow, shivers, and retreats to the warmth of his hearth. See ya next year, folks. "Beau says it's gonna to be an early spring!" the onlookers shout. The glad tidings are picked up by radio and TV stations across Georgia and the Southeast. If it's not a particularly urgent news day, Beau's upbeat forecast will be beamed all the way to California and Hawaii, where the natives first need to know: "What the heck is spring?"

Yellow River Game Ranch is at 4525 U.S. Highway 78/Stone Mountain Highway, Lilburn, about 20 miles east of downtown Atlanta. While you're at the ranch, pet, feed, and admire white-tail deer, Georgia black bears, bison, sheep, rabbits, goats, ducks, and other people-friendly critters grazing on the ranch's twenty-four acres. Admission fee. Phone (770) 972–6643 or (877) 972–6643, or check out www.yellowrivergame ranch.com.

The Big Chicken

Marietta

"Hang a right at the Big Chicken" . . . "Folks, you can't miss us, we're on 41, smack in front of the Big Chicken" . . . "Pardon the pun, folks, if you're seated on the right-hand side of the aircraft, you've got a bird's-eye view of the Big Chicken, one of the Atlanta area's most famous landmarks."

Londoners rendezvous by Big Ben; New Yorkers meet under the Grand Central Station clock. Since the early 1960s motorists navigating the highways of Marietta and Cobb County and pilots homing in on Dobbins Air Force Base and Atlanta-area airports have set their charts by a 56-foot, red-and-white sheet metal rooster that preens on the facade of a KFC outlet on busy U.S. Highway 41/North Cobb Parkway at Highway 120/Roswell Road.

The Big Chicken is much more than a big metal sign on a suburban Atlanta KFC. The big bird with the rolling eyes and flapping beak is a landmark that guides motorists and airplane pilots to their destinations.

The chicken was hatched in 1963 by S. R. "Tubby" Davis, who wanted a really big signature for Chick, Chuck and Shake, a fast-food joint he opened in a former peach orchard he purchased from a family named Frey. The big bird's original rolling eyes and flapping beak were shut down when neighbors complained that the noise kept them awake and scared the children. Heck, if he'd've been here during the Civil War, he'd've scared the Yankees back to Chattanooga.

Move forward into the 1970s. US 41—also known as "The Four-Lane Highway" because when it was built during World War II to facilitate the movement of Rosie the Riveters to the Bell Bomber Plant ("Bell Bummer" in the local lingo) it was the state's first, and for a real long time only, multilane thoroughfare—was the thruway for Yankee tourists high-balling it to Florida. The Big Chicken roped 'em in, and Tubby and friends put 'em back on the road happy and well greased. But I-75 came along in the late '70s, eclipsing the "Fo'-Lane" and siphoning off Tubby's clientele. KFC bought the place lock, stock, and chicken in 1980.

KFC's corporate suits, uncomfortable with their new store's maverick logo, had a potential "out" in 1993 when a tornado severely ruffled the big guy's feathers. They conducted a plebiscite in the Cobb County media, which asked (more or less): "Shall the advertising accouterment known as the Big Chicken be restored to his former glory, or shall he be sent to The Great Scrap Pile in the sky and be replaced by beautiful new signage identical to that of a zillion KFCs in 200 countries around the world?"

The vote was an overwhelming mandate, and the suits breathed a sigh as big as the twister that decimated the chicken. To show their solidarity with the citizenry, Colonel and Company spent $700,000 on the famous fowl's makeover.

"Taking it down would have been a PR nightmare for KFC," asserts Theresa Jenkins, executive director of the Marietta Welcome Center and Visitors Bureau. "And without the Chicken to show us the way, nobody around here would be able to get anywhere."

Viva El Pollo Grande!

The Big Chicken is at the intersection of US 41/Cobb Parkway and Highway 120/Roswell Road, Marietta, about 25 miles northwest of downtown Atlanta.

Moreland Loves Lewis
Moreland

The late humorist Lewis Grizzard would howl till he hurt if he could see his museum, which shares half of Coweta Monument Company, a tombstone maker. Lewis must be rolling around under his tombstone over this very bizarre, very grizzard, "housemate," alongside U.S. Highway 29 in his hometown of Moreland. Born in 1946 in the town of "400 or thereabouts" 40 miles south of Atlanta, the writer once described as "a Faulkner for plain folks" and "this generation's Mark Twain" went from here to become a folksy storyteller, stand-up comedian, newspaper columnist, and best-selling author. His daily column, originating in the *Atlanta Constitution,* was syndicated in 450 newspapers nationwide. His favorite topics were Georgia Bulldog football; his dog, Catfish; his mama; apple-pie patriotism; pickup trucks; barbecue; and the sweet, simple life of the fictional and factual folks back in Moreland. A shameless chauvinist, he even mined humor from his three failed marriages (such as the bumper sticker "Honk if You've Been Married to Lewis Grizzard"). He died of heart disease in 1994.

Grizzard's half of Coweta Monument showcases his worn-out Gucci loafers, high school letter jacket, photos, honors, and books: *When My Love Returns from the Ladies' Room, Will I Be Too Old to Care?*; *My Daddy Was a Pistol and I'm a Son of a Gun*; *Elvis Is Dead and I Don't Feel Too Good Myself*; and *Chili Dogs Always Bark at Night*. A videotape tribute characterizes him as a man for whom "life was always a party." When asked in the video about the glamorous life of a newspaper columnist, Grizzard quips: "Writing a daily column is like being married to a nymphomaniac. It's fun for the first two weeks."

The Lewis Grizzard Museum (2769 US 29; 770–254–2627) is open Thursday through Saturday. Admission $1.00. From I–85 take exit 35 and drive 3 miles south to Moreland and look for the museum sign in front of Coweta Monument on the right side of the highway. A section of I–85 in Coweta County is called "Lewis Grizzard Highway."

The Little Manse
Moreland

Morsel-size Moreland was the birthplace of another man of letters, even more famous—many would say more infamous—than Lewis Grizzard. Like Woodrow Wilson, Erskine Caldwell (1903–87) was the son of a Presbyterian minister and spent his early boyhood in the church-owned Little Manse, between Moreland and neighboring Luthersville. He was five or six years old when his father accepted another pulpit and moved the family away. By the time Caldwell wrote the steamy *God's Little Acre* and *Tobacco Road,* harpooning the tomcat morals of the Depression-era South, he was safely removed from the Bible Belt's outraged slings and arrows. In the 1940s he came back to his birthplace with his aged father and made a later, unannounced, visit, where he reportedly found his father's former church but not his boyhood Manse. No wonder he couldn't find it—the old homestead was a storage shed for livestock feed when it was rescued, moved to Moreland's town square in 1991, and restored as a museum. Times have definitely changed in the Bible Belt.

"Caldwell has always been controversial with Southerners," observes museum director Winston Skinner, who met Caldwell in 1982, five years before the author's death. "That hasn't totally ended, but there's much less antipathy now. The University of Georgia Press has republished several of his books, and there's renewed interest in his storytelling genius."

About 1,000 yearly visitors, including many church groups and students of American literature, come to see exhibits on Caldwell's life, his books in many languages, and his typewriter, clothing, wedding ring, and other personal effects.

The Little Manse is on Moreland's town square, off US 29, about two minutes from the Lewis Grizzard Museum. It's open Saturday and Sunday 1:00 to 4:00 P.M. and by appointment. Admission fee. Call The Manse (770–254–2627) or visit www.coweta.ga.us.

"With This Ring . . ."
Roswell

There's a big wedding in Roswell on December 22. Mittie Bulloch, a local debutante, will marry New Yorker Theodore Roosevelt in the dining room of Bulloch Hall, her family's Greek Revival showplace in the north Fulton County city, 20 miles north of Atlanta. Don't worry if you can't make it this year. Mittie and Theodore will pledge their troth again next year and the year after that, just as they've done for decades. The first time was in 1853, when the couple would have been flabbergasted at the far-reaching consequences of their union.

They moved to New York after the ceremony and in 1858 had a son, Theodore, who became our twenty-sixth president in 1901, when William McKinley was assassinated. Their other son, Elliott, became the father of Eleanor Roosevelt, who married her cousin Franklin.

In 1905, President TR made a sentimental journey to his mother's ancestral home. If he came back today, he'd find the house looking pretty much as it was when his mother was a blushing, eighteen-year-old bride. Mittie's father, Major James Archibald Bulloch, built the house in 1839, the same year Roswell King, a Connecticut Yankee, founded the town and built textile mills on the Chattahoochee River.

One of the South's rare examples of pure temple-form architecture, with a full pedimented portico, Bulloch Hall is one of more than 100 Roswell structures on the National Register of Historic Places. In 1978, the city of Roswell purchased the house and sixteen acres and opened it to the public. A few of the Bulloch family's original furnishings are complemented by period pieces. Modern brides say their vows in the dining room where Mittie said hers. A rerun of Mittie and Theodore's wedding is a high point of "Christmas in Roswell," which also features gobs of Victorian holiday décor, high teas, parades, seasonal music, storytelling, and the lighting of the town square.

Roswell King laid out his town in New England fashion, with a park in the center and a bandstand where TR spoke in 1905. Low-rise brick shop buildings around the square include an original general store, which sold everything but hard spirits. It now houses J. Christopher's, which serves breakfast and lunch, and still pours nothing more potent than sweet tea.

To arm yourselves with information on what to see and do, stop first at the Historic Roswell Visitors Center on the square, 617 Atlanta Street, (800) 776–7935, www.cvb.roswell.ga.us, for a video overview, historical exhibits, and walking tour maps. Guided walking tours depart the center on Wednesdays at 10:00 A.M. and Saturdays at 1:00 P.M. Bulloch Hall, 180 Bulloch Avenue, Roswell, (770) 992–1731, (800) 776–7935, is open daily. Admission fee.

The Lost Mill Workers
Roswell

Like all wars, the Civil War caught innocents unwittingly in the crosshairs. When Union troops occupied Roswell in July, 1864, they found some 400 women and children at Roswell Mills still making tent cloth for the Confederacy. Gen. Kenner Garrard reported to Union Commanding Gen. William T. Sherman, "The cotton factory was working at the time of its destruction, some 400 women being employed. I had all the buildings burnt."

That might have been the end of it, but Sherman was outraged and reported to the War Department in Washington, "I have ordered General Garrard to arrest for treason all owners and employees, foreign and native, of the Roswell Mills, and send them under guard to Marietta." And to Gen. Garrard, " I repeat my orders that you arrest all people, male and female, connected with these factories, no matter the clamor, and let them foot it under guard to Marietta [about 15 miles], then I will send them by cars [railroad] to the North."

To Southerners, the forced deportation and imprisonment of women, many of them with children, solidified Sherman's embodiment of absolute evil. Even Northerners were shocked. A New York newspaper wrote, "Only think of it! Four hundred weeping and terrified Ellens,

Susans, and Maggies transported in springless and seatless Army wagons, away from their loves and brothers of the sunny South, and all for the offense of weaving tent cloth."

The fate of most of the women was never known. Some who made their way back to Roswell years after the war found their husbands dead or remarried and other family members scattered.

The Lost Mill Workers Monument, in Old Mill Park in downtown Roswell, features a broken column that symbolizes the women's broken lives. Phone (800) 776–7935, www.cvb.roswell.ga.us. Rebuilt in 1882, the mill made textiles until 1975, when it was converted into offices and special event space.

Shrimp on the Mountain
Stone Mountain

Get out the barbie, mama, there's shrimp on top of Stone Mountain! But before you heat up the briquets, you'd best get your hands on a high-powered microscope and pray for a frog-strangling downpour. The "fairy shrimp" and "clam shrimp" that spawn on the 825-foot-high granite dome—in a 3,200-acre state park 16 miles east of downtown Atlanta—are hardly ever more than an eighth of an inch long. Adult shrimp lay their eggs in eroded cracks and crevices on the mountain and perish during hot, dry weather, when the granite heats up to more than 180 degrees. Come the rains and cooler temps of spring and fall, and the eggs hatch and perpetuate two varieties: "clam shrimp," encased in transparent shell, and shell-less "fairy shrimp." Yum-yum.

The seemingly barren rock's shallow pits also foster several types of wildflowers. Confederate yellow daisy (*Viguiera porteri*), which looks like yellow school bus paint spilled on the gray granite, is rare indeed. They grow only within a few-mile radius of the mountain and inspire the park's fall Yellow Daisy Festival.

The mountain's humpbacked gray dome rears up from the east Atlanta suburbs like Captain Ahab's worst nightmare. It began forming 200 million years ago when molten rock deep in the earth pushed close to the surface; eons and eons of soil erosion brought the world's largest granite monolith to the full light of day. Don't fret about a volcanic eruption spoiling your picnic—the rock's been silent since T-rex and company roamed these parts.

The location is better known for its giants than its shrimp. Confederate heroes Robert E. Lee, Stonewall Jackson, and Jefferson Davis gallop 90 feet high and 190 feet across the sheer north face—the world's largest outdoor sculpture. Workers on the carving—begun in 1925 and completed in 1970—could get out of the rain or heat inside a horse's ear or mouth.

I've eaten fried chicken in some peculiar places, but nothing can top May 1970, when I stood on the scaffolding in front of the finished carving with politicians and fellow journalists and tried to be nonchalant about a picnic on wobbly boards more than 800 feet above the ground. I remember the carving's fine details, patting the barn-size rump of Lee's horse, Traveler, and standing next to Bobby Lee's ear, taller than I am—but I don't remember a thing about the chicken and coleslaw.

Stone Mountain Park is on US 78/Stone Mountain Freeway, 16 miles east of downtown Atlanta. Call (770) 478–5600, (800) 317–2006, or log on to www.stonemountainpark.com. The park is open daily. Admission fee per vehicle.

Jefferson Davis, Robert E. Lee, and Stonewall Jackson ride on legless horses across the sheer escarpment of suburban Atlanta's Stone Mountain. When it rains, the mammoth granite dome gives birth to infinitesimal fairy and clam shrimp.

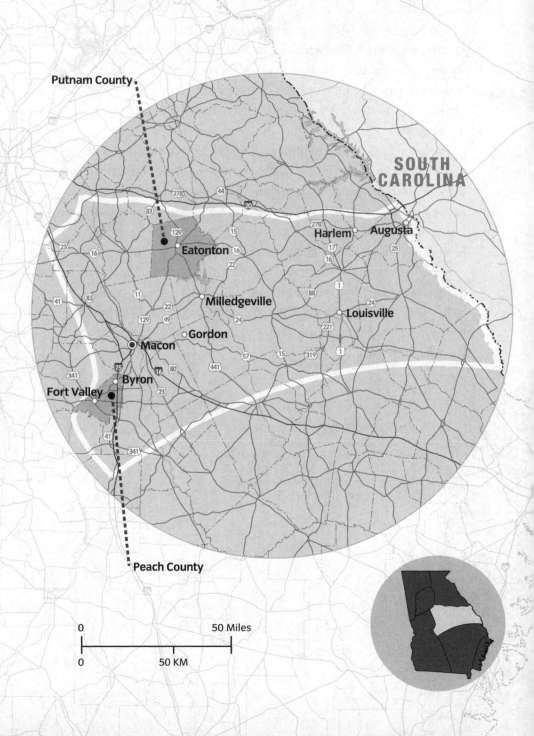

MIDDLE GEORGIA

Putnam County

SOUTH CAROLINA

278
44
83
20
129
15
Harlem
Augusta
Eatonton
278
23
16
486
17
25
22
16
11
Milledgeville
88
1
Louisville
83
22
24
41
129
49
24
221
Gordon
Macon
57
15
319
1
341
75
80
441
Byron
23
Fort Valley
341
41
341

Peach County

0   50 Miles

0   50 KM

MIDDLE GEORGIA

White-columned temples of old times not forgotten (look away, look away, Dixie Land) survive in the breadbasket of the state, which in these hipper times has spawned "Little Richard" Penniman, "Godfather of Soul" James Brown, Otis Redding, the Allman Brothers Band, and opera diva Jessye Norman, who started on the road to the Met as an Augusta gospel singer. Oliver Hardy was born here, and Duane Allman is buried here. Young Woodrow Wilson met Robert E. Lee in Augusta, met his first wife in Rome, and married her in Savannah. *Midnight in the Garden of Good and Evil*'s Jim Williams rests uneasily in Gordon. The literary world is also enriched by Eatonton's Joel Chandler Harris (*Tales of Uncle Remus*) and Alice Walker, Pulitzer Prize winner for *The Color Purple,* and by Milledgeville's Flannery O'Connor (*The Violent Bear It Away* and *Everything that Rises Must Converge*).

Fat Man's Forest and Cafe
Augusta

Like at Alice's Restaurant, you can get anything you want (nearly, any-way) at Fat Man's Forest. "We've got all kinds of stuff you don't need but just have to have anyway," smiles Carolyn Usry, who opened the Augusta bazaar with her late husband (aka "The Fat Man") in 1948. "Folks keep coming and taking stuff home, and we keep adding on more space for more stuff."

All that "stuff' includes wicker furniture and lawn chairs, artificial flowers, potted plants, Mexican pottery, piñatas, incense and candles (votive, voodoo, birthday, Hanukkah), Chinese toys, and tilde crockery and Augusta souvenirs "made in Taiwan." You'll also find pictures, posters, paper plates, pots and pans, T-shirts, Hawaiian shirts, U.S. flags and Rebel flags, caps and bumper stickers (HELL NO, WE AIN'T FORGOT),

Chef Purl Harris is the genius behind the squash casserole, bar-becued pork, catfish, fried chicken, and other ambrosial fare that puts a smile on the faces of her friends at Fat Man's Cafe in Augusta.

Carolyn Usry opened Fat Man's Forest in Augusta in 1948, selling everything from birthday party piñatas to St. Patrick's Day paraphernalia. She's also proprietress of Fat Man's Cafe, next door.

Augusta's hometown salsas and nachos, Christmas, Easter, and Halloween candy, and decorating stuff for every occasion. Augusta has a sizable Irish heritage, so around March 17 the place shimmers with emerald-hued St. Paddy's stuff. They've also got great stuff for Christmas, New Year's, July 4, and Memorial Day.

Come Halloween, you gotta take a number at Fat Man's costume department. Folks come from all over east Georgia and half of South Carolina (just across the Savannah River) to do themselves up as Bill, Hil, and Monica; Dubya and Cheney; Homer, Bart, and Marge; Biblical characters; and all-the-buzz movie, TV, and cartoon personalities. If you've seen 'em in *People*, you can be 'em for the night.

The maddening aromas that drift into the store can lay you nearly flat. While you still have strength, get on over to Fat Man's Cafe, a few yards from the Forest. The sign says it all: HOME OF PURL'S COOKIN'. JUST

GREAT CHOW. WE'RE WORKIN' ON THE SERVICE. Purl is chef de cuisine Purl Harris, who has been dishing up to-die-for squash and broccoli casserole, mac and cheese, candied yams, turnip and collard greens, stewed corn, rice and gravy, barbecued pork, liver and onions, catfish, fried chicken (natch), burgers and fries, banana pudding and Georgia peach cobbler (natch, natch), and other soul-satisfying fare since 1956. "The secret is in the grease," Chef Purl allows.

Fat Man's Forest is at 1545 Laney Walker Boulevard, Augusta; (706) 722–0796. Fat Man's Cafe is next door at 1717 Laney Walker Boulevard; (706) 733–1740, (800) 283–3287; www.fatmans.com.

Woodrow Wilson's Boyhood Home
Augusta

Woodrow Wilson left his mark on Augusta. Our future twenty-eighth president etched his first name, Tom, on a downstairs bedroom window and left scuff marks from his shoes under the dining room table. (He 'fessed up to the crimes during a visit many years later.) Wilson spent his boyhood in Augusta because in 1858 his father became pastor of Augusta's First Presbyterian Church and brought one-year-old Thomas Woodrow and the rest of the Wilson clan down from Virginia to a church-owned manse at 419 Seventh Street. Woodrow lived there longer than in any other house, including the White House, his address from 1913 to 1921.

Thomas Woodrow's thirteen years in Augusta—the family moved to South Carolina in 1870—gave him an enviable sheaf of show-and-tell. "My earliest recollection," he said in 1909, "is of standing at my father's gateway in Augusta, Georgia, when I was four years old and hearing someone pass by and say that Mr. Lincoln was elected and there was to be a war. I remember running in and asking my father what it meant."

As the war moved into Georgia, Woodrow got the answer up close and personal. He looked out his bedroom window at Confederate wounded and Union POWs on the grounds of his father's church. In 1865 he stood on a corner as Union troops escorted Confederate President Jefferson Davis (captured in southern Georgia) through Augusta's streets. Five years later he shook hands with Robert E. Lee, when the revered Southern icon was Augusta's honored guest. How long it was before he washed that anointed hand, he never said.

When he scuffed the dining room table, still in place in the parlor, he was probably just antsy to get outside and cut loose with some backyard baseball. His teammates on the Lightfoot Baseball Club, for which he wrote the constitution and bylaws, included next-door neighbor Joseph Rucker Lamar, a future U.S. Supreme Court justice, and another pal who became ambassador to Switzerland. Was it a touch of boyish impishness that prompted the Presbyterian minister's son to borrow the team's Red Devil logo from a popular brand of canned meat? Surely the lads weren't tempted by an advertising endorsement from one of their baseball heroes: "Nap Lajoie Chews Red Devil. Ask Him If He Don't."

Wilson was so fond of Georgia that he practiced law in Atlanta, fell in love with a Rome minister's daughter, and married her in Savannah. His daughter, Jesse, was born in a Gainesville hotel run by former Confederate Gen. James Longstreet. Then he went "Up North," as ambitious Southerners did, and found green pastures (president of Princeton, governor of New Jersey, U.S. president). He suffered a devastating stroke and died in 1924.

Wilson's boyhood home was rescued from life as a flower shop and beauty parlor in 2000 and reopened as a museum by Historic Augusta, Inc., in September 2001. "The day we closed the sale, women were sitting under beehive hair dryers in the dining room," recalls Erick Montgomery, Historic Augusta's executive director.

About a dozen pieces of furniture that belonged to the church during the Wilsons' tenure, including Woodrow's shoe-scuffed dining room table, have been returned to the house. The only item that belonged to the Wilsons is a butter dish, part of a silver service given to the family on their first Christmas in the house.

Woodrow Wilson's Boyhood Home is at 419 Seventh Street, downtown Augusta; (706) 724–0436, www.wilsonboyhoodhome.org. It's open for guided tours Tuesday through Saturday. Groups of ten or more should make an appointment. Admission fee.

"Save Our Butt"
Augusta

"Save Our Butt" may not have the patriotic eclat of "Remember the Alamo," but in 1997–98 Augustans rallied around their beloved Butt and saved the eighty-seven-year-old landmark from the scrap yard. Leonardo DiCaprio, Kate Winslet, and fellow travelers on the good ship *Titanic* were unwitting allies in the campaign that rescued the Archibald Butt Memorial Bridge from a fate as final as the great ship's.

Major Archibald Willingham Butt, a native Augustan and aide to President William Howard Taft, boarded the *Titanic* in 1912 for what proved to be history's most memorable inaugural voyage. When Big T was bushwhacked by the iceberg on the night of April 12, Major Butt helped scores of terrified women and children into lifeboats. He sank with the unsinkable liner, his body never recovered.

Two weeks after the disaster, President Taft came to Augusta to eulogize his fallen comrade: "I never knew how much he was to me until he was gone," the tearful Taft told the memorial service throng. He came back in 1914 to cut the ribbon opening the humpbacked little bridge that carried Fifteenth Street over the Augusta Canal.

Adorned with intricate ironwork, glass light globes, eagles, gilded masonry lions, and a memorial plaque to its namesake, the bridge (approximately 50 yards long) did its job faithfully and without fanfare until the early 1980s, when the Georgia Department of Transportation (boo, hiss) decided to take it out, like a bad tooth, to relieve Augusta's traffic pains. Into the fray marched a formidable array of naysayers.

"SAVE OUR BUTT MEMORIAL BRIDGE!" demanded bumper stickers distributed by the Butt Memorial Bridge Legal Defense Fund. The battle cry was echoed by politicos, everyday Augustans, and star-crossed *Titanic* sweethearts Leonardo and Kate (d.b.a. Jack and Rose), in absentia. Against such a juggernaut the embattled DOT scrambled for a way out. The movie *Titanic* turned the tide.

Victoria Forrest shows her support for the crusade that saved Augusta's beloved Butt Memorial Bridge from the hungry jaws of "progress." The bridge was named for Augusta native Major Archibald Butt. An aide to President William Howard Taft, Butt perished on the *Titanic*.

"The interest that has grown out of the film [1998's Oscar winner] is bigger than anybody would have guessed," observed Ross Snellings, an Augusta lawyer who founded the Legal Defense Fund. "A whole new generation now knows all about the *Titanic*, and this bridge is the only memorial to the disaster in Georgia. Now we've got Leonardo DiCaprio and Kate Winslet as ambassadors for the Butt Bridge." What ultimately saved Augusta's Butt was a plan to reroute some of the bridge traffic to another street and thus ease the congestion that had prompted the DOT to target the venerable bridge in the first place.

Here's the rest of the story: On April 15, 2000, the *Titanic* disaster's eighty-eighth anniversary, the pine trunk Major Butt brought onto the *Titanic*, one he'd carried into battle during the Spanish-American War, was auctioned by a Tacoma, Washington, antiques dealer. It sold for $6,000—about the price of Major Butt's one-way ride to Davy Jones' Locker. Butt Bridge is on Fifteenth Street, near downtown Augusta.

WASHINGTON'S DOG, R.I.P.

Did George Washington leave something precious behind when he visited Augusta in May 1791? Augusta historian Edwin Cashin believes there's truth to a long-rumored story that Washington's favorite greyhound, Cornwallis, died and was buried in what's now downtown Augusta.

In his book, *The Story of Augusta,* Cashin writes: "At some time during those three days, President Washington had the sad duty of burying his favorite greyhound. The episode wasn't mentioned at the time, but, according to an article in the *Augusta Chronicle,* in 1892 city workers unearthed a grave marker (near the intersection of Broad and 15th Streets) with the inscription, 'Here lies the dust of Cornwallis, the favorite of George Washington, whose recent visit to this colony shall ever be among its proudest memories.'" Cashin says that the epitaph explains a comment that appeared in the *Augusta Chronicle* (then, as now, the city's major newspaper) after Washington's death. Quoth the *Chronicle.* "His (Washington's) heart was as tender as a woman's, as those of us can testify who saw how the loss of a favorite pet could work upon his responsive feelings."

Skeptics believe the maybe-grave marker's disappearance throws cold water on the tale—a relic that important would almost certainly have been saved, they contend. And, says Erick Montgomery, director of Historic Augusta, Inc., "In 1791 what is now Broad and Fifteenth Streets was way out in the country. Nobody would have gone way out there to bury an animal. Washington was definitely here—Augusta was the state capital then—but I don't know if his dog was with him on that trip, or even if there was a dog. It could be a fish story, but a lot of people have swallowed it hook, line, and sinker."

The Petersburg Boats
Augusta

The Petersburg Boats, which carry sightseers on the Augusta Canal National Heritage Area, are named for the deceased town of Petersburg, whose remains are at the bottom of Clarks Hill Lake.

In the early 1800s, the town, at the confluence of the Savannah and Broad rivers, in modern-day Lincoln County, was the shipping point for farms and forests in east Georgia's back country. From there, the goods were shipped down the Savannah on long, narrow, flat-bottomed boats, 60 to 80 feet long and about 7 feet wide. The pilot, called a "patroon," and his six-man crew shot the rapids and collected cargo at plantation docks on the way to Augusta. There, it was loaded onto larger vessels for the downriver trip to Savannah. Three days were required to pull and pole the boats back to Petersburg, where the cycle began all over again.

Petersburg Boats, like this retro model, once carried nineteenth-century goods on the Augusta Canal, now a National Heritage Area.

When the Augusta Canal was built in 1845, the locks allowed the Petersburg Boats to avoid some of the most treacherous rapids on the way to Augusta. By 1877, at least twenty-five of the boats were plying the canal and the river. Gradually, rail and road transport replaced the Petersburg Boats, and by the early 1900s, most of them had disappeared. So had the town of Petersburg.

Patterned after drawings and vintage photos of the historic boats, today's Petersburg Boats carry passengers, not produce. Two boats, the *William Phillips* and *Henry Cumming*, named for early canal proponents, carry up to forty-nine passengers on narrated tours of the canal in downtown Augusta. Although their hulls appear to be wooden, like their predecessors, they are fiberglass, built at Tybee Island, near Savannah. They are also the largest electrically powered boats in the U.S.

Two hydropower engines inside the Interpretive Center at Enterprise Mill generate all the power for the massive former textile mill and the boats. The Augusta Canal is now a National Heritage Area. The wide towpath, once used by mules to pull canal boats to the headgates, is a popular recreational trail for hikers, cyclists, and runners. Trails into wooded and urban areas enhance the outdoor experience. Canoers and kayakers can put in at several points and enjoy the natural and urban scenery.

If you'd like to take a ride, visit the Augusta Canal Interpretive Center, Enterprise Mill, 1450 Greene Street, Augusta; (706) 823–0440, (888) 659–8926; www.augustacanal.com. Admission fee.

WHERE THE HECK AM I?

You can't tell a county by its county seat. Decatur is in Metro Atlanta's DeKalb County, but Decatur County (Bainbridge) nudges the Florida Panhandle. Forsyth is in Monroe County in the midsection, but Forsyth County (Cumming) is in northeast Georgia. Monroe is the seat of northeast's Walton County. Jefferson's in Jackson County, and Jackson's in Butts. Madison's in Morgan County, and Madison County's seat is Danielsville. Morgan is the seat of Calhoun County, in the deep southwest; Calhoun is the seat of Gordon in the far northwest; and Gordon is the largest town in Wilkinson in the middle. Roberta's in Crawford, and Crawfordville's in Taliaferro (Tolliver). Washington's in Wilkes, Sandersville in Washington. Macon is Bibb County's metropolis, but Macon County's miniopolis is Montezuma, named for the same American victory in the Mexican War that gave us "The Halls of. . . ." Hugh-ston is that big town in Texas—the middle Georgia county is How-ston. Vienna, in Dooly County, is a long way from Austria; so's the way it's pronounced Vigh (as in *sigh*)-enna. Cairo is *Kay-ro*, like the corn syrup. When in doubt, ask at the gas station down the road; when all else fails, consult a map.

What's Br'er Rabbit Up To Now?

Eatonton

He looks so innocent, standing there on the lawn of the Putnam County Courthouse in a smart red smoking jacket, white dress shirt, and blue necktie and holding a long-stemmed pipe. But anybody who's familiar with the pranks he's played on sly ol' Br'er Fox and dumb ol' Br'er Bear knows sure as the day's long that Br'er Rabbit's brain is always cooking up a devilish new scheme to pull on his gullible foils. Could "Tar Baby, the Sequel," be in the offing? He's there 24–7, in front of the courthouse on U.S. Highway 441.

Standing in front of the Putnam County Courthouse in Eatonton, Br'er Rabbit's got a studious look on his face. That could only mean more misery for Br'er Fox and Br'er Bear, the devilish Rabbit's favorite targets.

151

Joel Chandler Harris got his inspiration for Br'er Rabbit and his other critters from slaves on a pre–Civil War plantation near Eatonton. Harris left Eatonton as a boy and became an itinerant journalist. He settled in Atlanta in 1880 and wrote folksy stories from his childhood for the *Atlanta Constitution*. Over twenty-five years, nearly 200 of these charming tales were compiled into the nine volumes of Uncle Remus stories. The Uncle Remus Museum, a pair of joined-up slave cabins down the road from the courthouse (US 441; 706–485–6856; www.eatonton.com) exhibits first editions of his *Tales of Uncle Remus*, likenesses of his characters, and other antebellum standards.

RING THAT OLDEN BELL

In days of old, when Louisville (LEWIS-ville, named for King "Lewis" XVI of France) had a ten-year fling (1795–1805) as Georgia's capital city, the Old Market House in the center of Broad Street auctioned cotton, land tracts, collards, corn, and African slaves. The oak-beamed market is mostly silent these days, except for special occasions when its tower bell rings out. The bronze bell was supposed to be largesse from French King Louis XV to a convent in New Orleans, but in 1772 it was hijacked by pirates on the bounding main and ended up on an auction block in Savannah. The buyers packed it off to the capitol in Louisville, where it heralded American independence, slave auctions, Georgia's secession, and other major happenings.

Party Hardy
Harlem

Oliver Hardy came onto the world stage in 1892, in the teeny east Georgia town of Harlem. Teenage Ollie took the early 1900s version of the "A Train" out of Harlem and never looked back. He attended Georgia Military College at Milledgeville and the Atlanta Conservatory of Music and briefly studied law at the University of Georgia in Athens. But greasepaint was in his blood—he opened Milledgeville's first movie house and was so intrigued by silent films that he became a comic villain in a theater company. In 1918 Hardy followed his muse to Hollywood, where he was serendipitously paired with a young Englishman named Stan Laurel. Rotund fussbudget Hardy and gullible foil Laurel were a match made in the celluloid stars. Their comical mishaps, in more than one hundred films, kept the world laughing through the Great Depression and World War II.

They worked in radio, stage, and TV until Hardy went to cinema heaven in 1957. (Laurel followed a few years later.) Hardy's hometown (population 2,200) on the western fringes of Augusta, keeps his memory alive with a museum and annual festival.

Opened in 2002 in Harlem's old post office, the Laurel and Hardy Museum and Harlem Visitor Info Center is America's only museum devoted to the much-beloved comedians. Shelves are filled with the boys' photos, movie posters, pictures, and other keepsakes.

Laurel and Hardy classics like *Babes in Toyland* and *Sons of the Desert* are shown to groups and at the Laurel and Hardy Festival the first Saturday of October, when 30,000 fans trek from far and near to join parades, look-alike contests, and a street dance and enjoy good old-fashioned belly laughs as Ollie turns another situation into balderdash, wrings his derby like a chicken's neck, and fumes at Stan, "This is another fine mess you've gotten us into."

The Laurel and Hardy Museum & Harlem Visitor Info Center is at 250 North Louisville Street, Harlem. Phone (888) 288–9108 and (706) 556–0401, www.laurelandhardymuseum.org. Free admission. Take Interstate 20 exit 61, Harlem/Appling, and follow the signs to downtown Harlem.

The Great Yazoo Land Fraud
Louisville

Barring a little eighteenth century scandal, Georgia's boundaries might stretch westward to the Mississippi River. In 1795 state legislators, their palms heavily greased with bribes, sold 35 million acres of wild western lands along the Yazoo River to developers doing business as the Yazoo Companies. Even in an era of plentiful cheap land, the sales price was a shocker: $500,000 for the package, or about a cent and a half an acre. Outraged Georgians threw the rascals out of office, and the legislation and all the records pertaining thereto were burned on the state capitol grounds.

Legend says that as the bonfire was being readied, a white-haired gent on a coal-black horse galloped up and declared such an odious act could only be expunged by "fire from heaven." He beamed sunlight through a large magnifying glass and, poof, the papers were history. Not so, decreed the U.S. Supreme Court, which upheld the sale and paid off the land buyers. In 1802 Georgia put the mess behind it by ceding its lands west of the Chattahoochee River to the federal government. The states of Alabama and Mississippi were created from the bounty. To find out more, call the Jefferson County Chamber of Commerce at (478) 625–8134 or visit www.jeffersoncounty.org.

Down by the Riverside
Macon

Home from a heavy road trip, the Allman Brothers Band often revived their spirits with an all-nighter in Macon's Rose Hill Cemetery, winding down with brews and smokes, breezes off the Ocmulgee River, and a silent but appreciative audience of citizens and soldiers who populate the 150-year-old graveyard. So when band members Duane Allman and Berry Oakley were killed in separate 1971 and 1972 motorcycle accidents, they naturally came home to Rose Hill, where they rest side by side on a terrace with a river view. Duane's granite slab is etched with a guitar and scorpion, his Zodiac sign, and the inscription "I love being alive and I will be the best man I possibly can. I will take love wherever I find it and offer it to everyone who will take it. Seek knowledge from those wiser and teach those who wish to learn from me." Oakley's tomb bears an Aries ram, a guitar, and the admonition "Help thy brother's boat across, and lo! Thine own has reached the shore."

Duane Allman and Berry Oakley rest side by side in Macon's Rose Hill Cemetery. The members of the Allman Brothers Band died in separate motorcycle accidents in 1971 and 1972. Their fans still remember them with cigs and six-packs.

As in life the duo seldom want for companionship. So many faithful were leaving booze bottles, beer cans, and other tributes that a few years back a relative wrapped the grave site in a chain link fence topped with razor wire, to the horror of cemetery sextons, who swiftly pulled it down. Still, the pilgrims come, crayoning the stones with messages: "We Love U," "You Live 4-Ever," "Ramblin' Man keep on ramblin'," and dropping off cigs and six-packs.

The musicians aren't the only Rose Hill tenants who've left behind bons mots. Dr. J. J. Suber wants friends and family to know he's "Been Here and Gone—Had a Great Time." Lieutenant Bobby, a beloved brown terrier who got his army commission from his commander-in-chief, President Calvin Coolidge, had a wonderful life until he jumped down the elevator shaft of a Macon hotel and made a happy landing alongside his master in Rose Hill. Where there's dogs, little boys are bound to be nearby. John Ross Juhan wanted to be a fireman when he grew up, but when he died at age eight years, four months, and sixteen days, "The Brave Little Fireman's" headstone was sculpted with the fireman's coat, hat, and belt he proudly wore as mascot for Defiance Company No. 5.

Rose Hill Cemetery, 1091 Riverside Drive, near downtown Macon, is open daily during daylight hours. Call (478) 742–5084 or visit www.maconga.org.

Playboy in Braille

Macon

Guess he bought it just for the great feature stories. Blind country music singer Ronnie Milsap donated his June 1995 Braille edition of *Playboy* to the Georgia Music Hall of Fame, where it keeps company with such treasures as a photo capturing the meeting between "Godfather of Soul" James Brown and Holy Father of souls, Pope John Paul II. Audios and short movies showcase such diverse Peach State musical megastars as Lena Horne, Ray Charles, Travis Tritt, Jessye Norman, Otis Redding, "Little Richard" Penniman, and the Allman Brothers Band. You can purchase their CDs and cassettes in the gift shop, conveniently located on your way out. The Hall of Fame is located in downtown Macon at 200 Martin Luther King Jr. Boulevard; (478) 751–3334; www.gamusichall.com. Admission fee.

Bite-Fight Neckwear

Macon

The blood of both victors and vanquished "rusts" a black bow tie in a glass case at the Georgia Sports Hall of Fame in downtown Macon. Some of the most notorious blood spouted from the ear of Georgia's own Evander Holyfield when it was nearly severed from its mooring by Mike Tyson during the "bite fight" for the world's heavyweight championship in Las Vegas on June 28, 1997. Evander nearly forfeited his ear, but he retained his crown on a third-round disqualification. The bow tie was around the neck of veteran boxing referee Mills Lane, who struck a bargain for the trophy with the Sports Hall of Fame.

157

"When we were organizing the Hall of Fame a few years ago, we asked Mr. Lane if he could give us something connected to the fight," recollects Robbie Burns, the facility's public relations director. "He told us he had to wear the pants and shoes he had on that night for an upcoming fight, so he couldn't give us those. He had sold the shirt he was wearing to a man who offered him $200. But, he said, 'I'll make you a deal. Get me another bow tie and you can have the bite-fight tie.' My dad sent him a $10 tie from Penneys, and Mr. Lane sent us the bite-fight tie in exchange. He said that he'd worn that tie at every fight he'd reffed for the past fifteen or twenty years. He'd never had it cleaned, so it's got Holyfield's blood and who knows how many others." A Savannah native, Mills Lane has lived in Reno, Nevada, for many years, serving as a judge, attorney, referee, boxing promoter, and star of *Court TV*.

Just as the Otis Redding Memorial Bridge over the Ocmulgee River honors the Macon-born blues singer, who died in a 1967 plane crash before "Sittin' On the Dock of the Bay" made him an international celebrity, the Stribling Bridge honors another Maconite who died in a tragic accident before his destiny could be fulfilled. Born in Bainbridge, Georgia, in 1904, W. L. "Young" Stribling grew up and went to high school in Macon. In his short-lived fight career, he compiled an impressive record of 225 wins, 13 defeats, and 15 draws. Because he'd fight anyone, anywhere, legendary sports chronicler Damon Runyon nicknamed him "The King of the Canebrakes." He KOed 127 opponents, a record that stood until Archie Moore surpassed it in the 1950s. He held the world lightweight championship for all of three hours in 1923—until the referee, who'd been hired by his opponent, changed his decision and declared the fight a draw. Although he never weighed more than 190 pounds, Stribling moved up to the heavyweight class and reached his career zenith in 1931 in Cleveland. He fought Germany's Max Schmeling for the world heavyweight championship and lost on a technical knockout with fourteen seconds left in the fifteenth round. Two years later, Stribling was headed for a Macon hospital to see his wife and newborn child when his motorcycle crashed, inflicting fatal injuries. The fighter was so revered that 25,000 people paid their respects as his body lay in state in Macon's City Auditorium. He's been inducted into the International Boxing Hall of Fame, and boxing historians honor him as "the greatest fighter never to win a world championship." His gloves, photos, and other mementos are displayed in the boxing gallery of the Georgia Sports Hall of Fame, 301 Cherry Street, Macon. Admission fee. Call (478) 752–1585 or visit www.georgiasportshalloffame.com.

The Real McCoy
Macon

Dr. George Washington Carver is justly renowned for creating and cultivating hundreds of household items, from peanuts to soy beans, sweet potatoes, and other products. Much less heralded are nineteenth- and early-twentieth-century African Americans who patented many of the gadgets we take for granted every day. Their achievements are remembered in the Inventors Room at the Tubman African American Museum in downtown Macon.

When you're maneuvering your mower around the lawn on a hot summer day, say thanks to J. A. Burr, who created the forerunner to the riding mower in 1897, and J. S. Smith, who came up with the lawn sprinkler a year later. If you ever get an itch to play Captain Ahab, the barbed harpoon you'll hurl at hapless leviathans was the brainstorm of Lewis Temple, a freed slave who, sad to say, didn't patent his invention. You might be surprised that the gas mask and automated traffic signal are gifts of Garrett Morgan; the postal letter box, P. W. Downing; horseshoes, O. E. Brown; corn planter, J. W. West; fire extinguisher, T. J. Marshall; and ironing board, Sara Boone.

Lewis Latimer helped create the first electric lights; he was the only African-American member of the Edison Pioneers—Thomas Alva Edison's team of scientists. Granville T. Woods didn't work with "the Wizard of Menlo Park," but more than fifty electrified inventions won him the nickname "The Black Edison" all the same. In 1893 Dr. Daniel Hale Williams, a Chicago physician, performed the world's first successful open-heart surgery. Born a slave in Kentucky, Elijah McCoy invented a labor-saving device and gave his name to a popular phrase. His "drip cup" enabled railroad workers to add oil to locomotive machinery without shutting down the train. This and other innovations made him so famous that when people wanted the very best they demanded "the Real McCoy."

The Tubman African American Museum is at 340 Walnut Street in downtown Macon; (478) 743–8544; www.tubman museum.com. Admission fee.

ELIJAH McCOY
1843 – 1929

McCoy was an inventor whose parents had escaped from Kentucky. They fled to Canada, where Eli... ater they sent him to study engineering in ... He came back to the United States the on... s shoveling coal into railroad locomo... locomotives by hand was par... machinery so th...

Elijah McCoy's labor-saving device for locomotive machinery inspired the phrase, "The Real McCoy." McCoy and other African Americans, who patented everything from the riding lawn mower to the fire extinguisher and ironing board, are honored in the Inventors Room at Macon's Tubman African American Museum.

SWEET TEA

Like many other Southerners, Georgians make their iced tea ("ahs-tea") with a ratio of brewed-in sugar that can give the uninitiated a buzz intense enough to set off car alarms a block away. If you'd just as soon not trigger a panic, be sure to ask for your tea unsweet.

The Old Way at Nu-Way
Macon

Although the dictionary spells it "wiener," Nu-Way has spelled it "Weiner" and made it Macon's way since 1916, when Greek immigrant James Mallis opened his shoebox-shaped storefront at 430 Cotton Avenue and addicted Maconites to his private-label pork and beef franks in a steamed bun with mustard, onions, secret-recipe chili, and medium-wattage barbecue sauce. Three generations later, partners and cousins Spyros Dermatas and Jim Cacavias are doing their private label pork and beef "Weiners" the tried-and-true way in the original thirty-nine-seat diner, which has changed only marginally through the years, and ten other Macon and Middle Georgia outposts. Now the rest of creation knows what Macon has known all these years—that Nu-Way isn't just "the Best in Town," as its motto boasts. In the past few years, *Gourmet* magazine, *Southern Living, Money* magazine, and PBS have ranked Nu-Way's pups among the best from East Coast to Left Coast. And don't bring a lot of money. A fully dressed dog with chili-cheese fries and a soft drink served with Nu-Way's "Famous Flaky Ice" is a feast for little more than a "fin."

The original Nu-Way is at 430 Cotton Avenue at Cherry Street in downtown Macon; (478) 743–1366. It's open for breakfast and lunch Monday through Friday.

It's a Bird, It's a Plane . . .
Macon

Few pedestrians on downtown Macon's busy Cherry Street notice the small rectangular bronze plaque embedded in the sidewalk. Those who take the time to look are puzzled by the airplane propeller with the date, February 15, 1928. Only a few Maconites still recall that February afternoon when the sky fell on Cherry Street.

It was a cold winter day, sputtering snow, and many families were bundling up for the Southeastern Air Derby, which brought thirty of the country's most famous barnstormers to the city's Miller Field. Only a year after "Lucky Lindy's" non-stop Atlantic flight, aeroplanes were as rare in the skies over Macon as snow on middle Georgia's famous peaches.

At noon, pilot Samuel L. "Buck" Steele and copilot France "Lucky" Ashcraft were scheduled to promote the derby by flying over downtown and dropping three "noisemaker bombs" from 2,500 feet. A nationally known stunt flyer, Steele was scheduled to walk on his plane's wings, fly upside down, and parachute from 2,000 feet onto a target on the ground. Ashcraft was a student pilot.

"We went out on the front walk to watch them fly over and circle three or four times, dropping these bombs that were like fireworks," Mini Yetter Phillips told Ed Grisamore, a writer for *The Macon*

Telegraph, in a 1998 story commemorating the tragedy's seventieth anniversary. "I thought I saw one of the wings just float off. I remember saying, 'Golly I don't know how they did that. That's some trick.' Then my mama said, 'That's no trick, honey. He didn't mean to do it. It's going to fall.' And we watched the plane go down."

Howell Rankin, then age five, was playing with neighborhood friends.

"As kids, we were always looking up at the sky, because there weren't too many planes in those days. When a plane went over, it was something unusual. Sometimes the pilots would advertise by dropping candy bars out of the plane, tied with little red parachutes. We would wait for them to float down and grab them. Baby Ruths, that's what they were. That day, we heard him flying, and we all looked up and said, 'We're going to get some Baby Ruths coming down our way.'"

The bronze propeller embedded in a downtown Macon sidewalk recalls a winter morning in 1928, when the skies rained tragedy on Cherry Street.

But it was chaos, not candy, falling from the sky. "I can still see it clearly," Rankin recalled. "I can still hear the plane whining as it went to the ground."

Steele's plane went into a tailspin and nose-dived into the 500 block of Cherry Street. The front of the plane burrowed into the pavement, in front of a drug store and mercantile store. The engine was still running. The crash killed Steele and "Lucky" Ashcraft. A pedestrian, hit by flying debris, was decapitated when he ran out of Persons Drugs to see what was happening.

Mason Zuber, a nineteen-year-old driver for American Express Railway Company, was turning up Cherry Street when he saw the plane spiral to the ground two blocks from him.

"It was quite shocking and I got out of the truck and did what any nineteen-year-old boy would do. I reached into the wreckage and picked up Ashcraft's helmet and took it with me to the Railway Express office. My father was a depot agent there. When he found out what I did, he was so shocked, he took that helmet and threw it in the trash."

Among the injured bystanders was George Yetter, Sr., who was knocked down and tore ligaments in his knees.

"Knowing my daddy, he started running lickety-split down there when he saw the plane falling apart, and he was probably there by the time the plane hit the ground," Yetter's daughter, Mini Yetter Phillips, told Ed Grisamore in 1998. " He had to get down there on the front row."

Phillips still vividly recalled the afternoon when the sky fell on Cherry Street.

"When you see something like that, you never forget it."

Mrs. Lee's Rolling Pin and Other Relics
Macon

Nobody knows for sure how a wooden rolling pin that originally belonged to Mrs. Robert E. Lee ended up in a glass case at the Macon Confederate Museum, which adjoins the Cannonball House in downtown Macon's historic district. Curators of the museum are also loathe to speculate whether a long, wide crack in the pin resulted from its use on Bobby Lee's sainted noggin. A cream pitcher and a pair of French gilt chairs that once graced their Richmond ballroom are other Lee family mementos. Judge Asa Holt's 1853 Greek Revival house was nicknamed the Cannonball House during an 1864 Union attack on the city.

Did Mrs. Robert E. Lee ever use this wooden rolling pin on something more sensitive than pie crust? Sitting in a glass case at Macon's Confederate Museum, the pin loyally refuses to tattle on its famous family.

A twelve-pound Federal shell caromed off the sand sidewalk in front of the house, passed through a front porch column, then through a window into the front parlor, where it nearly felled the mistress of the house as she descended the stairs to investigate the ruckus. Fortunately for the lady, and her house, the shell was a nonexplosive variety; it's still bandied about by the house's docents. You can see it at 856 Mulberry Street; (478) 745–5982. Admission fee.

The docent at Macon's Cannonball House hefts a missile like the one that crashed into the foyer in 1864. Luckily, she wasn't there then.

Forget? Give Us Another Century or Two!

Milledgeville

When the Gothic-style Old State Capitol in Milledgeville—the state's capital city from 1803 to 1868—was restored to its antebellum splendor a few years ago, the Robert E. Lee chapter of the United Daughters of the Confederacy placed this plaque: "These grounds witnessed the greatest and most brilliant convocation ever held in the Commonwealth of Georgia, the Secession Convention of January 16–19, 1861."

When Sherman's Union troops occupied Milledgeville in November 1864, they held a mock session of the legislature in the capitol and "revoked" the Ordinance of Secession. Before they rode out of town, on the "March to the Sea" to Savannah, the troops burned the military arsenal, stabled their horses in St. Stephens Episcopal Church, stoked molasses down the church's organ pipes, and pulled a few more schoolboy pranks but otherwise left intact the only American city except Washington, D.C., planned specifically as a capital. Depending on which legend you choose to give credence, Sherman (1) found Milledgeville, like Madison and Savannah, too beautiful too burn; (2) had once courted a local beauty and didn't want to distress her by burning down her family's manse (if Billy Sherman courted even half the belles attributed to him from Louisiana to Virginia, he'd've had precious little time to make war hell, as he so loved to do); (3) was a devout Mason, dissuaded from destruction by brothers of the Baldwin County lodge. Closer to the truth is that, like Madison and Savannah, Milledgeville had no military importance, and Sherman decided to save his torches for rural plantations and other targets vital to the war effort.

The Old Capitol is at 201 East Greene Street; (453) 478–1803. The graceful, arched entrance gates were built after the war from stones salvaged from the destroyed military arsenal. It's now a classroom building for Georgia Military College. The House Chamber, where the 1861 Ordinance of Secession was approved (and "revoked"), is open Monday through Saturday.

Where's the Dome?

Milledgeville

The Old Governors Mansion gets my vote as the state's most beautiful public building. It's a no-brainer, really. Even architectural historians consider the elegant mansion, built in 1838, to be one of America's most outstanding Greek Revival residences. Fronted with four Ionic columns supporting a pediment and hipped roof, the stucco-covered brick house was painted a muted pink, described at the time as "mellow rose, the color of a lovely pink-tinged sunset, just deepening into crimson." This being Middle Georgia, most who see it say that it's peach. From 1839 to 1868 the mansion was the home of ten Georgia chief executives—and an uninvited guest named Sherman.

Architect Charles B. Cluskey designed the mansion with a central rotunda and dome inspired by Palladio's Villa Rotonda in Vicenza, Italy. The 40-foot dome, which floods the rotunda with natural light, is so ingenuously designed that it can't be seen from the street. John Linley, in his book *Georgia Catalog: A Guide to the Architecture of the State*, asserts that "the Governor's Mansion in Milledgeville is probably the finest Thomas Jefferson–inspired design outside of Virginia." He says it's similar to plans Jefferson drew, but never carried out, for the Virginia governor's mansion in Richmond and the president's house (White House) in Washington, D.C. In its heyday before the Civil War, the mansion's high-ceilinged rooms, with French wallpaper, heart-pine floors, crystal chandeliers, and French Empire, Federal, and English Regency furnishings, were the scene of galas and balls thrown for dignitaries who traveled to the remote capital from Washington City and other far-away places. As Sherman's Union army approached the city in November 1864, the governor fled with carts laden with the mansion's furnishings, leaving Sherman to sleep on an army cot in the empty ballroom. Some of the furnishings failed to return from exile; others were "lost" during the capital's move to Atlanta in 1868. With their raison d'être gone, the mansion's grand rooms became a dormitory for the state women's college across the street. In 1967 the students moved out, and the house was restored as a historic site and home for the president of what's now Georgia College and State University.

Completed in 1838, the Old Governor's Mansion in Milledgeville was home to ten chief executives and a party-crasher named William T. Sherman. The Greek Revival showplace recently underwent an attic-to-basement restoration to its glory days of the 1850s.

In April 2005, a three-year, $9-million restoration returned the mansion to its 1850s grandeur. Funded by the Georgia General assembly, the Woodruff Foundation, and private donations, the project has restored the original layout, color scheme, and overall appearance of the building. The interior of the dome has been regilded and the picket fence around the grounds reproduced from old drawings. Behind the scenes, it also received new mechanical and electrical systems and a new roof. A new education building includes a visitor center and a museum store.

The Old Governor's Mansion is at South Clarke and West Greene Streets, Milledgeville; phone (478) 445–5004, (800) 342–0471; www.gcsu.edu/mansion. The mansion is open for individual and group tours Tuesday through Sunday. Admission fee.

Flannery's Literary Legacy

Milledgeville

An aspiring novelist once asked Flannery O'Connor if she thought that journalism schools stifled creativity. "Not nearly enough," she shot back, with her typical in-your-face humor. "No telling how many bestsellers could be prevented by more diligent teachers." Flannery O'Connor achieved international literary acclaim without ever darkening a journalism school's doors and rarely venturing beyond Milledgeville. Born in 1925 to Catholic parents in Savannah, five-year-old Mary Flannery got her first glimpse of the limelight when Pathe News featured her and her backward-walking pet chicken in a newsreel shown in movie theaters around the country. (Hey, the Depression was on and people were scratching around for every laugh they could get.)

The family moved to Milledgeville when O'Connor was thirteen. After she graduated from Georgia State College for Women, now Georgia College and State University in Milledgeville's historic district, in 1945, she was a writer the rest of her life; she never married and never held a "real" job. She sequestered herself at Andalusia, her family's dairy farm on the outskirts of town, and wrote two novels, *Wise Blood* and *The Violent Bear It Away*, and two short-story collections. She drew most of her Southern Gothic characters and bizarre plot lines from people and situations she saw around her. It was a popular pastime among her neighbors to try to discern who in their circle was weird enough to be the model for Hazel Motes, Francis Marion Tarwater, Rayber, the Greenleafs, The Misfit, Rev. Bevel Summers, Mr. Shiftlet, Mr. Paradise, General Sash and his daughter Sally Poker Sash, and other rascals, revivalists, backwoods meanies, freaks, and patient sufferers she brought to life. "My characters aren't grotesque," she told a writers' workshop; "it's just the way Southern people are." She was right. I run into them all the time.

O'Connor died of disseminated lupus—the same incurable disease of the immune system that killed her father—in August 1964, four months short of her fortieth birthday. Her manuscripts, letters, typewriter, copies of her books in many languages, paintings she did as a hobby, including a self-portrait, and other personal items were willed to the Flannery O'Connor Memorial Room at Georgia College's Ina Dillard Russell Library. A short film tells the story of her life. When school's in session, the library is open Monday through Friday. Call (478) 445–4047 or visit www.library.gcsu.edu. Fans can visit O'Connor's grave site in Memory Hill Cemetery on Franklin Street, two blocks from the college.

Alas, Poor Jim
Gordon

While Danny Hansford lives it up with the silk-stocking crowd in Savannah's Bonaventure Cemetery, Jim Williams, Danny's *Midnight in the Garden of Good and Evil* companion, the man who done him wrong, is 200 miles away, and I imagine not very happy about his change of fortune. The flamboyant art and antiques dealer, social arbiter and Savannah's host with the most, lies under a black granite marker in the yard of Ramah Primitive Baptist Church (Old Line), near his rural hometown of Gordon, 20 miles east of Macon. Oh, how the fastidious Mr. Jim must abhor his straight-laced companions, few of whom would likely know Spode from a snow shovel. Wouldn't he love to get his manicured hands on whoever keeps putting pots of plastic flowers on his resting place? But, just in case he gets any notions about going back to his days of wine and Rose Medallion, his mama's right there beside him, ready to rein him in.

Where, oh, where is Jim Williams? The protagonist in *Midnight in the Garden of Good and Evil* is in a quiet, middle Georgia churchyard, far from the scene of the crime and victim Danny Hansford.

Ramah Primitive Baptist Church is on Highway 57, between Macon and Irwinton. Williams's black granite grave marker is on the left side of the cemetery.

Miss Katherine, Flannery O'Connor, and Sam Walker
Milledgeville

The late Miss Katherine Scott is one my most unforgettable characters. I met her for the first time in 1974, when a magazine sent a photographer and me to spend a night with Miss Katherine and a ghost that spooked her Milledgeville home. With a halo of snowy white hair and a natural flair for hair-raising storytelling, she was the kindly grandmother we all wish we had. She'd shared her house with a tormented wraith for all of her more than seven decades.

When her papa returned from the Indian Wars on the Great Plains in the late 1800s, he purchased the 1830s house on North Jefferson Street. The bang-for-the-bucks included a mansard roof, French windows, rose gardens, and the spirit of Sam Walker.

"People nowadays do a lot worse things and nobody pays 'em much mind," she said, "but back a century or so ago around Milledgeville, Sam Walker was known as the wickedest man in Georgia. They said he had murdered several black people, cheated other people out of money, and all kinds of other evil deeds. Papa told me this story. A demon down in Hades saw Satan sitting on a big upside down wash pot. He asked him why he was sitting there, instead of out corrupting more souls. Satan said, 'I've got Sam Walker under this washpot, and I'm afraid if I turn him loose, he'll take over this whole place.'"

Walker's most notorious malfeasance led to the death of his only son, and literally haunted him the rest of his life.

"His son, Josiah, came home from Mercer College in Macon with an infectious fever. He needed a doctor, but black-hearted Sam wouldn't hear of it—he said Josiah was faking his illness to get out of work on the family farm. He even refused his wife's pleas for so much as a drink of water to cool the boy's fever. Finally, after a couple of days, Sam went to see for himself. When he got to the bottom of those stairs over there, Josiah came out on the landing, glassy-eyed and soaked with the fever.

"'Papa, you see I'm really sick,' he whispered, then he collapsed and tumbled down the stairs and landed in a heap at his father's feet. Sam yelled for a doctor, but it was too late. The boy was dead, and the fever killed his mother not long after."

Pretty soon, Josiah began a series of special appearances. Sam saw him so often at the top of the stairs, he had the upstairs closed off. He saw him at the foot of his bed in the dead of night, and by day on the streets, at card games, and at saloons. Sam saw him on his deathbed and pleaded, in vain, for forgiveness.

As the photographer and I were getting ready to retire, our hostess said, "Sam was cursed to walk these steps until the end of eternity, or until the house falls down, whichever comes first. To this day, you can hear his footsteps and a thud, as though Josiah is once again dying at his father's feet."

With those comforting thoughts, I mounted the steps to sleep in Josiah's four-poster deathbed. The wee hours were like a Vincent Price movie. Rain fell in torrents, thunder crashed, lightning flashed, the old house creaked and groaned, a grandfather clock bonged the quarter hours. Then I heard it—a heavy tread resounded on the stairs, then another and another. Something crashed onto the floor downstairs. The footsteps seemed to be coming closer. The grandfather clock announced 3:00 A.M. Then all was silent. I didn't get up to investigate and didn't emerge from under the quilts until the sun was well up.

"I guess you heard Sam doing his mischief last night," Miss Katherine said with a knowing smile. "See, the rascal threw that picture on the floor. The hook's still in the wall."

The photographer was awake all night in the downstairs room next to hers. He heard the ghostly footfalls and vowed the lady of the house didn't make the ghostly bumps in the night. When he processed his pictures, a vaporous image with a human shape was clearly visible at the top of the stairs. Josiah, is that you behind those Foster Grants?

On a lighter note, Miss Katherine had taught English for many years at Milledgeville's State College for Women, now Georgia College and State University. She wasn't at all pleased at the way her tutelage influenced her most famous pupil.

"I read one of her books" she bristled, "and Flannery [O'Connor] could have done the world a big favor by killing off that odious main character on the first page instead of waiting to the end of the book. Flannery was a genius—warped, but a genius, all the same."

The next time I saw Miss Katherine, she was sharing another antebellum house with a woman named Franny Wicks (not her real name), who was an outpatient at the state mental hospital and given to bursts of eccentric behavior. Miss Katherine recounted a time when her housemate put on a fur coat, and nothing else, in the middle of August, withdrew a large amount of money from a bank, and handed out cash to flabbergasted pedestrians on downtown sidewalks. While she was telling me about this old house's resident spooks, and pointing out precious antiques, including a dining table she said once belonged to King Louis XV's mistress, Madame Pompadour, she paused at a blank space on the wall, thought a few seconds and *hmm*-ed. "Franny Wicks, what have you done with that Rembrandt?"

SLAVERY LINKS

When you've visited Flannery O'Connor's grave, left of the main gates, look over in a corner of Memory Hill Cemetery, where "slavery time" graves are marked by iron hooks with links of chain. One link marks the graves of those born into slavery. Two links means the person buried there was born and lived in slavery. Three links designates the grave of someone who was born, lived, and died a slave. Opened in the early 1800s, the tree-shaded graveyard is the resting place of several Georgia governors and Revolutionary and Civil War soldiers.

Bob and the Big Peach

Peach County

South of Macon, any doubts that this is serious peach country are vanquished at the sight of "The Big Peach." Standing on a pedestal at I–75 exit 149/Highway 49, the whopping-big peach measures 75 feet from leafy stem to pointy tip and a bulbous 28 feet in diameter. Fashioned from an aluminum frame laid over with a vinyl-covered canvas hoopskirt, the peach was put up in 1985 to call motorists' attention to the Big Peach Antique Mall (119 Peach Parkway; 478–956–6256), where you can find all kinds of great stuff you never before realized you needed but have to have right now.

If you drop by the Byron Depot, in the rescued 1870 choo-choo station at 101 East Heritage Boulevard, you can learn a lot about old-timey trains and see some old-timers on the tracks. In late April and early May, the staff at the Byron Convention & Visitors Bureau and Welcome Center will encourage you to meet "BOB." That's an acronym for the "Battle of Byron," two weekends when friends and neighbors, tourists, and others who just happen by challenge one another to feats of skill and daring, including bubble gum blowing, 30-yard dash, three-legged race, Frisbee toss, arm wrestling, hula hoops, and mud pit volleyball. When you've been hosed down, join the parade, sock hop, barbecue, square dancing, gospel singing, pet show, and golf and softball tournaments. For more information you can contact the center at 100 West Heritage Boulevard; (478) 956–2409 or (888) 686–3496; www.byronga.com.

Can I Have Mine A La Mode?

Peach County

In honor of the Georgia Peach Festival, "Georgia's Official Food Festival," the good folks in Peach County, epicenter of the Peach State's peach industry, whip up the "World's Largest Peach Cobbler." If your town would like to match it, here's your challenge: Assemble 90 pounds of margarine, 32 gallons of milk, 250 pounds of sugar, 300 pounds of flour, and 75 gallons of sliced, succulent Peach County peaches. (Peaches from South Carolina, California, or some other foreign place just won't work.) Then set up a concrete-block oven and propane burners under a big tent. Round up every able body you can catch and set a 6-by-9-foot stainless-steel pan on said oven. Add the ingredients; stir and mix thoroughly. Light the propane burners and bake the cobbler eight hours or so. Get yourself a big jug of sweet tea, relax in the shade, and enjoy the Peach Hat Contest, the street dance, and other festivities. When the cobbler's ready, give a shout and hand out free samples of the bubbling Georgia ambrosia as long as it lasts, which won't be very long. When the last morsel's gone down, get everybody you can catch to help load everything on trucks for the trip home. After that, you're on your own. Spend the next day washing the pans and mixing apparatus.

If you don't want to miss out on next year's Peach Festival, contact the Peach County Chamber of Commerce, (478) 825–3733, www.peachcountyga.com. The two days of fun, the first weekend of June, are divided between the Peach County towns of Byron and Fort Valley, I–75 exit 149/Highway 49.

Big Birds
Putnam County

If the Rock Eagle could fly, he'd be as big as a small plane. Measuring 102 feet from wingtip to wingtip and 102 feet from head to tail, on a mound 10 feet high, this really big bird of prey was created as a Native American ceremonial icon some 5,000 to 6,000 years ago. The prone eagle's thousands of baseball-to-boulder-size pieces of milky quartz were laboriously hauled long distances without aid of wheels or beasts of burden. If it's really as ancient as archaeologists believe, the eagle may be twice as old as Egypt's pyramids. A message on a marker at the base of the effigy was left by a Creek chieftain in more recent centuries: "Tread softly here, white man, for long ere you came, strange races lived, fought, and loved." To appreciate the effigy's dimensions and pristine beauty, climb up the stone tower built in 1937, and view it from three stories high.

After admiring Rock Eagle, drive on down to Lake Oconee and see its bigger, less-well-known brother, the Rock Hawk. Probably built by the same prehistoric hands that created Rock Eagle, the granite-and-quartz hawk measures 132 feet from wingtip to wingtip and 102 feet from head to tail. University of Georgia archaeologists who dug trenches around the hawk in the 1950s failed to unearth clues to its origin. There's no tower to view it from above, so bring your imagination.

To see Rock Eagle, take Interstate 20 exit 441/129/Madison/Eatonton, and drive south. Rock Eagle Effigy is in the 1,452-acre Rock Eagle State 4-H Center, 9 miles north of Eatonton; (706) 484–2800; www.eatonton.com. Amenities include public picnic grounds and a fishing and boating lake. Open daylight hours. To reach Rock Hawk from Rock Eagle, drive 9 miles south on US 441 to Eatonton, then go east on Highway 16 for about 12 miles to the entrance to Georgia Power Company's Lawrence Shoals Recreation Area at 125 Wallace Dam Road; (706) 485–5494.

NORTHWEST GEORGIA

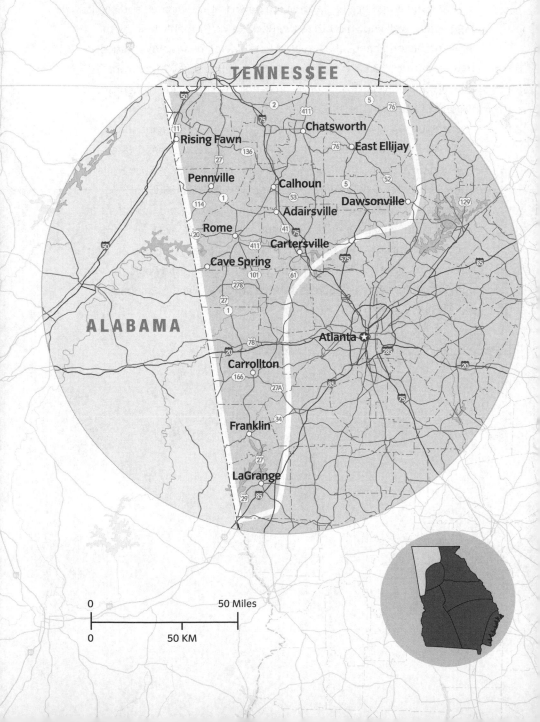

TENNESSEE

Rising Fawn

Chatsworth

East Ellijay

Pennville

Calhoun

Adairsville

Dawsonville

Rome

ALABAMA

Cartersville

Cave Spring

Atlanta

Carrollton

Franklin

LaGrange

0   50 Miles
0   50 KM

Northwest Georgia

In this hillbound corner, bumped against Tennessee and Alabama, you can visit Susan Hayward, at peace in Carrollton. There's a mob of kangaroos in Dawson County, and Mussolini's scandalous gift and Henry Ford's largesse are up front in Rome. You can achieve immortality on Ellijay's Pig Hill of Fame and salute dear friend Lafayette in LaGrange. The Appalachians are winding down here, smaller than in northeast Georgia and not as given over to tourism. You can follow wilderness trails through mountainous national forests, deep gorges, and waterfalls; explore a limestone cavern in Cave Spring; and swim in a pool shaped like the map of Georgia. And in the fall, when northeast Georgia's mountain roads are gridlocked with leaf-peepers from Atlanta, the WELCOME sign is usually out at the northwest's country inns and state parks.

Godfrey and Julia, Together Forever
Adairsville

Like the tortured spirits of Cathy and Heathcliff in *Wuthering Heights*, some believe that the ghosts of Englishman Godfrey Barnsley and his Savannah wife, Julia, still wander the ruins of their Italianate villa on the grounds of the Barnsley Inn and Golf Resort at Adairsville. Godfrey arrived penniless in Savannah from England in the 1820s and in a few years was a wealthy cotton broker, claiming as his bride Julia Scarbrough, daughter of the shipping family that sent the first steamship across the Atlantic. To save his bride from tuberculosis, Godfrey purchased 10,000 acres in former northwest Georgia Indian lands and began building an elaborate brick manor house, surrounded by formal

Do the ghosts of Godfrey and Julia Barnsley still visit the ruins of their manor house near Adairsville? There are those who swear they've seen these long-departed in the house and formal gardens, now part of the Barnsley Inn and Golf Resort.

gardens. The bracing mountain air was no miracle drug for poor Julia—she died in 1845, before the house was finished. But she was one determined lady; it's said that her apparition guided Godfrey in the manor's completion.

The Union army drank up the wine cellar and made off with the silver, but the house survived the Civil War, only to be left a melancholy shell by a tornado in 1906. In recent years a Bavarian prince has converted the area around the ruins into a luxury resort with golf, a European spa, and a German beer garden. But Godfrey and his Julia are still occasionally sighted walking among their boxwood parterre, spooning by a fountain embellished with an image of Julia.

Barnsley Gardens is 10 miles west of Interstate 75 exit 306. Call (770) 773–7480 or (877) 773–2447 or visit www.barnsleyresort.com.

It Sure Beats Smoke Signals
Calhoun

On February 21, 1828, journalistic history was made at New Echota, capital of the Cherokee Nation, when its print shop published the first issue of the *Cherokee Phoenix,* the world's first Native American newspaper. The paper relayed the news with an alphabet developed by a tribal scholar named Sequoyah. Born George Guest, Sequoyah was the son of an Indian trader of Dutch ancestry and a Cherokee mother. A silversmith as a young man, Sequoyah asked a friend to write his name so that he could create a die to stamp his work. He became curious about the white man's written language, so-called "talking leaves," and spent more than a decade developing a written alphabet, or syllabary, for the Cherokees. What he came up with was a system that used symbols that represented monosyllables of the Cherokee spoken language. He marked a total of eighty-five symbols on a piece of bark and showed it to skeptical tribal leaders, who were won over when Sequoyah demonstrated how he could communicate with his children by using the symbols.

The *Cherokee Phoenix* was published from 1828 to 1832 by Elias Boudinot. After the Cherokees were expelled from Georgia during the late-1830s "Trail of Tears," the print shop, courthouse, taverns, stores, and other buildings were burned or torn down and the land parceled off to white settlers. Many buildings have been reconstructed, including the print shop, where a press similar to Boudinot's original produces copies of the *Phoenix* for visitors.

New Echota State Historic Site is on Highway 225, 1 mile east of I–75 exit 317. Admission fee. A film at the visitor center tells the tragic story of the Cherokees. Call (706) 624–1321 or visit www.gastate parks.org.

Pass me the sports section, please. In 1828, a part-Cherokee named Sequoyah developed a written alphabet that was used in the publication of the world's first Native American newspaper. The re-created printshop is at the New Echota State Historic Site, at Calhoun.

Susan Sleeps Here

Carrollton

Among the gravestones of a tiny Catholic church on Carrollton's Center-point Road are those reading F. EATON CHALKLEY, 1909–1966 and MRS. F. E. CHALKLEY, 1917–1975, and the inscription, I AM THE RESURRECTION AND THE LIFE. A smaller marker is a bit more informative, saying GRAVE OF SUSAN HAYWARD CHALKLEY.

In 1957 glamorous film star Susan Hayward met Floyd Eaton Chalkley, a Carrollton automobile dealer and landowner, at a Hollywood party. Miss Hayward had several times mentioned to friends her "weakness for Southern men," and the tall, dashing, Southern-gentlemanly Chalkley fit the criteria. Just like a movie romance, they fell in love, eloped, and assumed a mostly quiet married life on Chalkley's large property outside Carrollton, where they raised cattle and horses and tried to be regular folks in the mostly rural community. (Carroll County in the late 1950s had a population of about 35,000; with Metro Atlanta pushing in from the east, it now counts more than twice that many.) "Susan was from Brook-lyn," says Jonathan Dorsey of the Carrollton Convention & Visitors Bureau, "but she was quoted as saying that she never had a hometown until she moved here. She liked the fact that Carrolltonians let her be a neighbor. She could shop on the square in curlers and nobody paid her much attention. But they certainly knew who she was. When she won the Best Actress Oscar for *I Want to Live* in 1959, she left the Oscar cere-mony in the middle of the night and flew back to Carrollton, where she was given a hometown welcome on the square."

When Eaton Chalkley died of liver disease in 1966, Hayward fled memories and moved to California and Florida. Her own end was near—in 1972 she was diagnosed with multiple brain tumors. She col-lapsed after cohosting the 1974 Academy Award Ceremonies and died on March 14, 1975. In accordance with her wishes, she was buried beside her husband in the cemetery of Our Lady of Perpetual Help Catholic Church in Carrollton, built on property they had donated across from the gate to their home. In a somber replay of the triumphal parade that welcomed her home with her Oscar in 1959, thousands lined the 7-mile route from the funeral home to the church.

As a grim epilogue to her story, several years after her death macabre facts began to emerge. Four of her costars in the so-bad-it's-good movie *The Conqueror* also died of cancer. They included John Wayne, who portrayed Genghis Khan in his career's most bizarre role, and veteran actors Agnes Moorehead and Dick Powell. Several other cast members and technicians who worked on the film were also afflicted. During the 1954 filming, the area around St. George, Utah, was fanned by radiation from eighty-seven aboveground atomic blasts in the nearby southern Nevada desert. A study also revealed that children born in southern Utah in the 1950s died of leukemia at a rate two-and-a-half times greater than those born before the atomic tests.

The gravesite at Our Lady of Perpetual Help Catholic Church, 210 Centerpoint Road/Highway 113, is open all the time. For information contact the Carrollton Area Convention & Visitors Bureau; (770) 214–9746 or (800) 292–0871; www.visitcarrollton.com.

I'll Have Mine 4-Way

Cartersville

If your neighborhood diner was bashed by a tornado or burned to cinders and the owner lacked the wherewithal to put it back together, would you pitch in to put your favorite comfort food back on the counter?

You'd probably dig into your pockets, maybe even rob your kids' piggy banks, if the diner was as beloved as Cartersville's 4-Way Lunch. After midnight on June 29, 1993, a rare Cartersvillian still on the streets of this city of 15,000 spotted flames shooting from the fire-engine red, sixty-two-year-old downtown landmark. Firefighters, many of them 4-Way faithful, rushed to the scene, but the little wood-frame structure suffered grievous damage. As the rubble cooled, bad news drifted from the blackened shell: Owner Ernest Garrison, whose father opened the place in 1931, had no insurance or money to start over. Devastated at the loss of the counter crew's joshing camaraderie as they set down plates of burgers, hot dogs, and fries sloppy with onion gravy and chili beans—and dismayed by thoughts of mornings without eggs, biscuits, and grits swimming in pork-sausage drippings—friends of the 4-Way responded to the SOS. Electricians and carpenters worked for free; suppliers donated food and equipment. Donations poured in from Atlanta (50 miles south) and as far away as the Carolinas and the Midwest.

Would you mind splashing on just a little more of that gravy? That tangy onion gravy doled onto burgers, dogs, and fries keeps the eleven seats at 4-Way Lunch in Cartersville perpetually filled. With a brief "fire break" in 1993, 4-Way's been Cartersville's way since 1931.

Two months after the disaster, it was business as usual—and it's been that way ever since. From 5:30 A.M. when the doors open, to midafternoon when they close, the diner's eleven stools are filled with lawyers, doctors, ditchdiggers, cops, clerks, city hall and county courthouse minions, housewives, kids, and tourists shunning I–75's fast-food glut.

The onion gravy's still as tangy, the experience just as rich as it's always been. If you've been in a few times, they'll put in your "usual"' as soon as you show your face and will ask about your kids, your job, your trip to Gatlinburg. It's all very friendly, but there's a caveat behind the Formica counter: "This isn't Burger King. You don't get it your way; you get it our way, or you don't get the damn thing."

4-Way Lunch is at Main and Gilmer Streets in downtown Cartersville; no phone. From I–75 take exit 288/Cartersville Main Street and drive five minutes. You can't miss it—it's the bright red shack on the left as you come into town.

Booth Western Art Museum
Cartersville

It's surprising enough to find one of the newest and largest repositories of American Western art in the "wilds" of northwest Georgia. The Booth Western Art Museum, in downtown Cartersville, exhibits more than 250 paintings and sculptures by America's leading contemporary Western artists, and others who dabbled in the genre. (Pop artist Andy Warhol did a screenprint of John Wayne; sports artist Leroy Neiman, a psychedelic mixed media of those Western sports, Lone Ranger and Tonto).

The Presidential Gallery is the museum's biggest surprise. How did the museum in this small town manage to collect an original signed document of all forty-three U.S. Presidents, and exhibit each one with a portrait or photograph? Internationally renowned photographer Yousuf

Karsh took the photos of presidents Herbert Hoover, Dwight Eisenhower, John F. Kennedy, Lyndon Johnson, Richard Nixon, Gerald Ford, Ronald Reagan, George H. W. Bush, Bill Clinton, and Jimmy Carter.

Some of the documents deal with official matters of state. Washington writes his secretary of war about an ongoing problem with the stubborn British, who just wouldn't accept the end of the affair. Lincoln queries the attorney general about an army hanging of thirty-nine Western Indians. Citizens often give their chief executives credit for knowing the most minute minutiae. In 1904, the editor of *The Ladies Home Journal* asked Grover Cleveland (1885–1889 and 1893–1897) "to settle the question as to how a little girl should salute the flag." To which Cleveland replied, "I am always glad to aid in matters of this kind that smack of patriotism; but in this particular case I confess I am at wits' end, and beg you to excuse me from making any suggestion on the subject."

Cleveland was out of office and had no aide, or inclination, to research the question. If he had, he could've replied that the proper flag etiquette was for the girl to place her right hand, palm open, over

The Booth Western Art Museum, in downtown Cartersville, exhibits an extraordinary collection of paintings, sculpture, Western pop art, and presidential letters.

her heart. With his typical Irish wit, John F. Kennedy, campaigning for president in 1960, thanked the publisher of Grove Press "for sending me so topical and practical a campaign manual as Edward Sorel's *How to Be President*. Though I am only a bench observer, it's most helpful to have this rule book on the Presidential game."

Like their subjects, the chief execs had day-to-day personal problems as well. Writing his stockbroker, thirteenth president Millard Fillmore (1850–53) exclaimed, "Cannot believe the velocity with which my portfolio has descended."

With only four years at the public trough, Fillmore had reason to be concerned.

The Booth Western Art Museum is at 501 Museum Drive, Cartersville. Call (770) 387–1300 or visit www.boothmuseum.org.

Spelunking in Cave Spring
Cave Spring

You've heard of New Mexico's Carlsbad Caverns and Mammoth Cave in Kentucky, but unless you're from around northwest Georgia or northeast Alabama, you've probably never heard of Cave Spring's cave. The scale is somewhat different: It'd be a crevice, lost in a corner of those labyrinthine national monuments. But for this area it's something special. From inside the limestone cavern—barely big enough to squeeze in half a dozen average size humans at a time—a sweet spring flows into a tree-shaded pond, askim with ducks and surrounded by gracious old trees. Around the pond is Rolater Park, the gift of a long-ago citizen, with picnic table pavilions. Next to the park is a 1.5-acre swimming pool, shaped like a map of Georgia. Encircling the park and pool is the village of Cave Spring, with 950 residents, a single traffic light, and more antiques and gift shops per capita than any other place in Georgia

I can think of. While you're browsing the shops, do your sweet tooth a favor—pick up a sackful of just-made fudge at Martha Jane's Fudge, Gifts and Collectibles (706–777–3586), then go sit in the park and toss cracker crumbs to the little guys in the pond.

Cave Spring is on U.S. Highway 441, 12 miles south of Rome and a few hops and a couple of steps from Alabama. For information call Cave Spring's City Hall at (706) 777–3382 or visit www.romegeorgia.com/cavespg.html.

The Mystery Wall
Chatsworth

Did twelfth century Welsh adventurers wander into northwest Georgia four centuries before Chris Columbus sailed the ocean blue? Did Hernando DeSoto and his merry band of Spanish conquistadores camp out on the slopes of Fort Mountain as they made their way to Memphis and the Mississippi? Just who did build the enigmatic rock wall that snakes 885 feet along the summit of Fort Mountain, 7 feet at its highest and 12 feet at its widest?

In 1782 John Sevier, a Revolutionary War hero and first governor of Tennessee, wrote about a conversation with ninety-year-old Cherokee chief Oconosto, who purportedly told Sevier that the wall's builders were "a people called Welsh, who had crossed the Great Water." Their leader was called Modok. Tantalizingly, Welsh legends tell of a Welsh prince named Madoc, who sailed away in the late twelfth century and was never heard from again. Other theories claim that the wall was built as a ritual site by light-skinned Indians named Madogs, or that it was "busywork" for DeSoto's restless troops, anxious to get to Memphis and see Elvis. Maybe Cherokees put it up to ward off their enemies, the Creeks. Your guess is as good as the experts'. Without

Modok's charm bracelet, or another smoking gun, the wall will remain a whodunit shrouded in mystery as soupy as the fog that often shrouds the mountain.

Fort Mountain State Park is on Highway 52, about 10 miles east of the I–75 exit 52, Walnut Avenue/Dalton. A walking trail goes to the mystery wall. Call (706) 695–2621 or (800) 864–PARK for campsite and cottage reservations or visit www.gastateparks.org. There's a parking charge.

Jumpin' Jimminy!
Dawsonville

Scarlett O'Hara's Aunt Pittypat might exclaim, "Kanga-roos in Jaw-ja! How ev-ah did they get heah!" Elementary, my dear Pitty: Debbie and Roger Nelson brought their 'roos and other Down Under critters to an eighty-seven-acre northwest Georgia outback at the end of the last century. They breed the largest collection of the hip-hopping marsupials outside Australia—200 and counting—and other curious creatures for zoos and wildlife sanctuaries as far away as China. We're invited to come see how it's done.

During the two-hour tour, you can imagine you're in the middle of Aussie nowhere. Kangaroo "mobs"—as groups of them are called— hop up close to the bright-yellow army truck and gaze at you with big soulful eyes. Newborn "joeys" peek from mama's pouch. The kanga-roos, weighing 150 pounds or more, dwarf the center's other inhabi-tants, such as the lovable little dik-dik, a miniature East African antelope no bigger than a house cat. They're on the endangered list, but kanga-roos are not—their gestation period is thirty-seven days.

The Kangaroo Conservation Center is at 222 Bailey-Waters Road, Daw-sonville; (706) 265–6100; www.kangaroocenter.com. Visits are by reser-vation Friday through Sunday, April through November. Admission fee.

Travis Brady, a trainer at the Kangaroo Conservation Center in Dawsonville, shows one of his "prize pupils" to Victoria Forrest of Dunwoody. "Can I take him home?"

Fast Track City Hall
Dawsonville

No drab institutional architecture, yellowing portraits of hizzoners long forgotten, or dull historical plaques grace Dawsonville's City Hall. In the heart of north Georgia's NASCAR Country—home of legendary champion Bill Elliott ("Awesome Bill from Dawsonville") and other celebrated drivers—city hall in this mountain town of 850, seat of rapidly growing Dawson County, population about 15,000, is decked out with checkered flags, trophies, plaques honoring racing legends, souped-up moonshine runners, and lean, mean racing machines only a few seasons from the big-time NASCAR tracks.

When Thunder Road, a racing attraction far from the nearest interstate, failed in 2004, the city bought the building at a taxpayer-pleasing price and moved its offices in among the racing memorabilia.

"We have one of the most unique city halls in the world," says town clerk Kim Cornelison. "People doing business with the city, and NASCAR fans from elsewhere, can walk through a reopened Georgia Racing Hall of Fame. The Alleyway area has cars driven by Dawsonville's own Gober Sosbee and Raymond Parks and a test car with a virtual reality screen. It's a great way to show off our city's heritage."

When visitors work up an appetite, they can tuck into Southern comfort food at Champions Café.

The Mountain Moonshine festival, on the town square in late October, commemorates the industry that sustained the populace during the Great Depression and spawned hell-for-leather drivers, who frustrated the "revenooers" and set the foundation for today's NASCAR mania. The festival's namesake is absent, officially, at least. Dawsonville City Hall is at 415 Highway 53 East, Dawsonville; (706) 265–3256.

MURDER AND MISS MAYHAYLEY

On an eccentric character scale of 1 to 10, Mayhayley Lancaster would have registered about a 25. Well known to folks around Heard County, who came to her to have their fortunes told and "signs" read, "Miss Mayhayley" (1875–1955) became a national celebrity when she stole the show at the sensational 1948 "Burned Bones" murder trial of wealthy farmer John Wallace. Her fame spiked again when Newnan author Margaret Ann Barnes turned the trial into the nonfiction best seller, *Murder in Coweta County,* made into a 1980s made-for-TV movie with Andy Griffith as murderous John Wallace; Johnny Cash as the righteous sheriff who brings him to trial for the murder of his tenant farmer, Wilson Turner; and June Carter Cash as the gaunt, rheumy-eyed, all-seeing Mayhayley.

During the trial, Miss Mayhayley testified that she told Wallace she could see Turner's body in a well on Wallace's property and that Wallace later moved the body from the well and burned it in a swamp. Turner's burnt bones were discovered, and Wallace went to the electric chair for the crime, just as Mayhayley predicted.

After the trial Miss Mayhayley made a killing from tourists, who braved her rundown shack's rotting cotton bales and packs of dogs to have their fortunes told. She'd sit in a rocking chair, in a ragged shawl and baseball cap, and fall into a trance to find a missing cow or runaway spouse or look into the supplicant's future. Mistrustful of banks, she planted the loot she earned beneath the planks of her house, buried in fruit jars and fertilizer sacks. Chickens laid their eggs in nests of stashed cash.

When she died in 1955, her fame followed her to the grave. Vandals so severely damaged her headstone that it was taken for safekeeping and public display to the Heard County Historical Center Museum, an early-1900s Romanesque Revival jail, which housed miscreants from 1912 to 1964. Carved on the shattered stone, a Biblical inscription from John 7:15 was directed at her detractors: FOR NEITHER DID HIS BRETHERIN BELIEVE IN HIM. The museum is at 151 Shady Street, on Franklin's courthouse square; (706) 675–6507. Information is also available at the Heard County Chamber of Commerce at (888) 331–0560 and www.heardgeorgia.org.

These Little Piggies
East Ellijay

The first little piggy went up in 1989. In need of an eye-grabbing gimmick to draw customers into his Real Pit Barbecue, the Rev. Colonel Oscar Poole made little plywood porkers, painted them with family members' names, and stuck 'em on a hill behind his sunshine-yellow establishment of the barbecuing arts. Pretty soon, folks around Ellijay and others driving past wanted to be immortalized on what soon became known as Col. Poole's Pig Hill of Fame. Oscar happily complied, asking only a donation for Methodist missions (he's a minister as well as a barbecue impresario). Today, the pen on the hill has close to 2,000 wooden piggies, and newcomers are always welcome to join the club. When you drop by to get your personalized sow or boar up there, tuck into a plate of Oscar's 'cue and Brunswick stew. It's pretty darned tasty.

Poole's Real Pit Barbecue and Pig Hill of Fame is on Highway 515 in East Ellijay; (706) 276–1700. Open daily.

Decked out in his pig regalia, the Rev. Colonel Oscar Poole proudly shows off his customized "Pig Mobile." Behind him, 2,000 signed plywood piggies graze on the Pig Hill of Fame, at Poole's Real Pit Barbecue in East Ellijay.

Lafayette, You Are Here
LaGrange

In the center of town, the place of honor Southern towns traditionally reserve for heroes-in-gray of the Late Unpleasantness, LaGrange has the noble Marquis de Lafayette. The story goes that as the beloved Frenchman's 1825 farewell-to-America tour bumped and bruised through wild west Georgia's wilderness, only recently appropriated from the Creek Nation, the homesick hero of our Revolution observed to one of his hosts that the countryside hereabouts reminded him of LaGrange, his estate across the sea.

The homesick Marquis de Lafayette had no way of knowing that a chance remark in the west Georgia wilderness would centuries later put him atop a fountain, in a square named for him, in a town named for his estate back in France.

Mon Dieu! Georgians were thrilled to hear their hardscrabble homeland likened to such cultivated country, so when Troup County was created a year after the Marquis's passage, naming the county seat LaGrange (French for "the barn") was a no-brainer.

As part of LaGrange's 1976 bicentennial observance, the city's downtown park was christened Lafayette Square and centered with a fountain, encircling a bronze likeness of himself precisely like the one in his hometown of LePuy. Lafayette Square is smack in the middle of LaGrange (population 25,000), on U.S. 27/I–85, 60 miles west of Atlanta. If you're venturing westward into Alabama, check with Humphrey Bogart for letters of transit.

Brother Howard Has Left This Earth
Pennville

Howard Finster has gone to a higher calling. The "Man of Vision" the Smithsonian and many others hailed as America's greatest living folk artist died in October 2001, but he left behind an incredible legacy. Finster's uniquely surreal, quite often bizarre paintings and sculptures have graced the Smithsonian, the Library of Congress, and museums and galleries from New York to California. Atlanta's High Museum of Art has a cache of 164 of his best works. He did Swatch watch faces and album covers for rock groups R.E.M. and Talking Heads. R.E.M. recorded the video for "Radio Free Europe" at Paradise Garden, Finster's 2.5-acre art compound near Summerville.

An avowed teetotaler, Finster agreed to do a poster for Absolut Vodka on the stipulation that he could include a temperance message. He played his harmonica and told Gospel homilies on the *Tonight Show with Johnny Carson*, leaving the usually gabby host speechless. He painted Coca-Cola bottles 14 feet high, splashed with hundreds of faces; crafted a tower of bicycle parts; and created other outsize sculptures and paintings that commanded major bucks. But the bulk of his more than 50,000 works were inexpensive plywood sculptures, 6 to 10 inches high, featuring angels, birds, frogs, heaven-bound buses, happy clouds, and likenesses of Marilyn Monroe, Elvis, Einstein, George Washington, Henry Ford, Abe Lincoln, Hank Williams, Martin Luther King Jr., and his own self-image. He signed all the pieces and included spiritual messages such as: "Angels Are from God, Believe in Them," "God Measures Your Soul from Top to Bottom," and "This Life Is Too Short to Stumble Around over God's Holy Bible into Hell's Fire."

It all began in the early 1960s, when, Finster said, a divine vision told him he could be of better service as an artist than as a preacher and bicycle repairman. He had had other visions: When he was three years old, he said that his deceased sister visited him in a tomato patch. He saw Elvis—and Adolf Hitler: "I told him, 'Hitler, you're a fool.'"

His funeral was a celebrity send-off. PBS, CNN, and the *National Geographic* covered

The late folk artist Howard Finster poses with two of his favorite subjects: a plywood self-portrait as a young man and an angel, both inscribed with biblical admonitions. In his long career, Finster created thousands of paintings and sculptures, many of them in museums, galleries, and private collections across the country.

Surreal smiley-faces, with biblical homilies, are part of the legacy of the late folk artist Howard Finster. His paintings, wooden sculptures, and esoterica are exhibited at Paradise Garden, near Summerville, and at Atlanta's High Museum of Art.

the services, attended by family, friends, and fans who wore Finster's brightly colored ties with happy-face clouds. They cried and sang "Amazing Grace," but as much as he was loved, Finster didn't get all his final wishes. He was buried in a churchyard, not his templelike structure at Paradise Gardens, and not in the casket he decorated with the advertisement for the funeral home that donated it—hornets had built a nest in it, and family members decided that they'd best leave 'em be. Undaunted by the minor inconvenience of his passing, Howard is still there in, um, spirit at Summerville's mid-May Finster Fest.

Paradise Garden, on U.S. Highway 27 at Pennville, north of Summerville, is open daily. Call (706) 857–2926 or (800) 346–7837, or visit www.finster.com. The High Museum of Art's Finster collection is at 1280 Peachtree Street, Atlanta; (404) 733–4444. Admission fee.

Is a Name Just a Name?

Rising Fawn

Georgia has many evocative place names—Flowery Branch, Fair Oaks, Pine Log, Chestnut Mountain, Holly Springs, Doerun, Deerwood, Parrott, and scores of others conjure pleasant thoughts of the nature they were named for. But when I hear the name Rising Fawn, I imagine a foggy morning, eons past, when a newborn Bambi rose from his mama's flanks and wobbled on his own feet for the very first time. "What is this place, how will I survive here?" the youngling might well have asked himself as he raced back to mama's comforting licks.

If you believe in legends, that's how this little community on the side of Lookout Mountain, in Georgia's far northwest corner, got its name. Cherokees, who inhabited the steep ridges and green valleys of Lookout Mountain centuries before Europeans found their way here, customarily named their children for the first thing they saw after the newborn's birth. And so it was that a tribal chief stepped out of his lodge at first light and saw a fawn rise from its mother side, stretch its legs, and behold his new world. Rising Fawn, he called his babe. When white settlers who came to the remote area in the 1830s heard the legend, they named a town for it. I think it's one of the most beautiful names for a town I've ever heard, anywhere.

Rising Fawn's setting is as enchanting as its name. The community sits on the doorstep of Cloudland Canyon State Park, a fitting name for the magnificent 2,300 acres sitting close to the clouds on the rugged, woodsy rim of Lookout Mountain. Serene and peaceful now, the area has endured a stormy past. During the Late Unpleasantness, 40,000 Union troops rampaged through here—devouring all the livestock and forcing the local folk to hide in caves—on their way to a bloody destiny at nearby Chickamauga and Chattanooga. After the war northern industrialists built an iron ore smelter, and Rising Fawn's population zoomed to close to 2,000, with a weekly newspaper, shops, a dance hall, a whiskey distillery, and a brass band that played for the citizens' edification. The smelter soon went bust, and today, if all the heads were counted on farms and rural routes served by the tiny Rising Fawn Post Office—known wryly hereabouts as "the Federal Building"—the population probably wouldn't top 200 or so.

But don't go feeling bad for Rising Fawners who have to drive an hour to Chattanooga for a Whopper. Some foggy morning, they just might look out and see the spirit of a newborn fawn rising to its feet, smelling life for the very first time. Take I–75 exit 320 and Highway 136 to Lafayette, then go 18 miles west on 136. You'll know you're in Rising Fawn when you see the entrance to Cloudland Canyon State Park.

The village of Rising Fawn sleeps beneath the morning fog that blankets Lookout Mountain in far northwest Georgia. A Cherokee legend inspired the village's picturesque name.

> # HAIR HEAVEN, WHERE EVERY HEAD WANTS TO GO
>
> (Sign on a home beauty shop on U.S. Highway 411 between Chatsworth and Ranger)

Mussolini's Gift
Rome

Never look an Italian dictator's gift in the mouth (you might get bit). In 1929, when Italian-owned textile mills provided paychecks to hundreds of Depression-era Rome, Georgians, Benito Mussolini sent the city a goodwill gift. Il Duce was pleased as penne pasta that the little northwest Georgia town was named for his glorious capital. It was, although quite by chance. In 1834 two traveling salesmen and a cotton planter put their choice of names in a hat. When "Rome" was pulled, people said, "Whattaya know? We got a bunch of hills just like Rome over yonder and three rivers instead of one puny Tiber. Good thing Warsaw or Hamburg didn't come outta that hat."

Anyhow, when city fathers uncrated Il Duce's offering, they were flummoxed, to say the least. Well-mannered Southern gentlemen, they smiled politely, said "thankyaverymuch," and put the bronze replica of the Capitoline she-wolf suckling infant Romulus and Remus (ancient Rome's mythological founders) on display in front of City Hall—then ran for cover. *Lupus canis* weathered a stormy decade. Worldly Romans thought it gave the town a touch of class. The not-so-worldly pinned teats and tykes with diapers and shielded their children's eyes. When Il Duce teamed up with Adolf, city officials had an excuse to put mama and the kids under cover for the duration of hostilities.

In these more-enlightened times, the little family sits bold-as-bronze, shameless and diaperless in broad daylight, downtown on Broad Street in front of City Hall. Most everybody in the city of 40,000 thinks it's just fine—or doesn't think about it much at all. There are holdouts, to be sure.

Blame it on Benito. In 1920s Georgia, a woman nursing her children in public was an embarrassment—even if mom was a wolf and her twins were the mythological founders of ancient Rome.

One morning when I was photographing the statue a bleary-eyed citizen of the streets wobbled up and watched with obvious disdain.

"I ain't believing none of it, " he announced.

"How's that?" I replied.

"I ain't believing no dog ever nursed no human kids," he said firmly. "It ain't happened. No, sir, never did."

Having set the record straight, he cocked his head and careened into Broad Street, oblivious to honking horns and shaking fists, still muttering boozy curses at those of us too ignorant to know that no dog ever nursed no human pups. Find out more from the Greater Rome Convention & Visitors Bureau; (800) 444–1834; www.romegeorgia.com.

Miss Berry and Mr. Ford

Rome

The story goes that In 1900, when Martha Berry was raising money for Berry Schools at Rome, she encountered Henry Ford on a very bad hair day. Tired of being hit on by every charity in the country, the cantankerous automaker reached into his pockets, grabbed a handful of change, and flung it across the desk, telling Miss Berry: "This is all the money I've got in my pockets. Take it and leave."

Unfazed by the rude treatment, Miss Berry pocketed the tycoon's spare change—87 cents—said thankyaverymuch, and returned to Rome and purchased seeds. A year later she went back to Ford with photos of the gardens, trees, and crops she'd planted with his "gift." Ford was so impressed that he wrote her a check for $25,000 and in 1924 he financed the school's Ford Complex, a cluster of seven English Gothic buildings and a reflecting pool. When the college celebrated its one-hundredth anniversary in 2002, it got a $9.4-million birthday grant from the Ford Foundation.

Set on 28,000 wooded acres—the world's biggest college campus—Berry began as an educational "leg up" for impoverished Appalachian youngsters. From Miss Berry's tiny seeds, it has grown into what *U.S. News & World Report* says is the South's number-one comprehensive undergraduate college. About 85 percent of its 2,100 students work around the campus for all or part of their tuition. The tight-fisted Mr. Ford would be mighty pleased to see the fruits of his investment. "The Miracle of the Mountains," as the college's story is known, is told at the campus's Martha Berry Museum; (706) 291–1883 or (800) 220–5504; www.berry.edu/oakhill. Oak Hill, Miss Berry's Family's Antebellum home, is open to visitors.

Berry College coeds, in antebellum finery, conduct guests through the Greek Revival home of the college's founder, Martha Berry.

COUNTING COUNTIES

Georgia's 159 counties are second in number only to Texas, which comprises 254 counties in an area four times our size (57,919 square miles versus 261,914 square miles). In the nineteenth century the state legislature decreed that all citizens should be within a half-day's horseback ride from a courthouse so that they could get there, do their voting, unhitch their spouse, sue their neighbors, etc., and ride home for supper in the same day. Many of our counties are so small you can toss a cow chip from one end to the other and so thinly populated you wouldn't hit anybody if you did. But the total area of the three biggest—Ware, Burke, and Clinch, with 2,565 square miles—is greater than the whole state of Delaware's 2,489 square miles. Like "The Sorcerer's Apprentice" in Disney's *Fantasia,* the courthouse mill kept grinding counties out into the 1920s, when many farmfolk had already switched from Flicka to flivvers. The last one debuted in 1924, when someone pointed out that we had counties named for bacon and coffee but none for our signature crop. So Peach County was created from ribs of Macon and Houston Counties. There'd be 161, but two bellied-up during the Great Depression and threw in with Atlanta's Fulton County.

SOUTHEAST GEORGIA

SOUTH CAROLINA

Twin City

East Dublin

Metter

Hawkinsville
Eastman
Vidalia
Chauncey
McRae
Claxton

Glennville

Fitzgerald
Irwinville

Waycross

Ashburn

Okefenokee
Swamp

FLORIDA

0   25 Miles

0   25 KM

SOUTHEAST GEORGIA

South of Interstate 16 and east of Interstate 75, this region is most reminiscent of the "old Georgia" that has vanished in other parts of the state. It's thinly populated, dotted with swamps and dense pine forests, and agriculture is still the mainstay. "Sweet" Vidalia onions grow here and nowhere else. Moultrie is Georgia's "Tobacco Road," and in our Dublin you can find the Redneck Games and compete in armpit serenading, hubcap hurling, and mud pit belly flopping. You can be a rattlesnake cowboy in Claxton, see the Statue of Liberty in McRae, and visit the world's biggest cricket farm in Glennville. Valdosta (50,000) and Waycross (20,000) are southeast Georgia's big cities, but leave your passport at home when you make the grand tour of Milan, Dublin, Scotland, Santa Claus, Seville, Jerusalem, Queensland, Eldorado, Rhine, and Waterloo. And let me know if you solve the mystery of Enigma.

Crime and Punishment
Ashburn

Normally, you need to commit a crime to spend time in jail. At Ashburn's Crime and Punishment Museum, all you have to do is surrender the admission price. Built in 1906, at a cost of $10,000, and known by inmates and Turner Countians as "Castle Turner," for its ornate Romanesque architecture, the jail housed inmates upstairs and jailers and their family lived downstairs. On the "business end" of the jail visitors can enter the original cells, the death cell, the hanging hook, and the trap door, where two felons at a time could be hanged.

Jailers and their families kept the grounds so attractively landscaped, travelers sometimes mistook it for a hotel. After the tour, visitors are invited into The Last Meal Café, where Southern-style food is served in the family's former living quarters.

Georgia has long record of severe punishment for criminal malfeasance. The 1930s film, *I Was a Fugitive from a Georgia Chain Gang*, with John Garfield as the escapee, brought the whole sordid system to light. The first person legally executed in the state—when it wasn't a state, but a British colony—is believed to be Alice Ryley, an Irish immigrant indentured servant, who was hanged in 1735 for murdering her master, Will Wise. Hangings continued until 1924, when the Georgia General Assembly substituted the electric chair as a more "humane" means of capital punishment. Lethal injection is now the legal method.

Thomas Alva Edison, who gave the world the electric light, the phonograph, and other conveniences, also invented the electric chair. He calculated it could dispatch a man in five seconds. However, after witnessing the chair in action, and seeing that it required up to four minutes of steady current to do the job, Edison regretted his invention the rest of his life.

The Crime and Punishment Museum and The Last Meal Café are at 241 East College Avenue, Ashburn. Call (800) 471–9696, (229) 567–9696 or visit www.turnerchamber.com. Admission fee.

CALLING ALL FIRE ANTS

The Fire Ant Calling Contest is one of most anticipated events of Ashburn's late March Fire Ant Festival. Calling the vicious little pests doesn't require any skill. "You can call 'em any way you want," festival organizers say, "but if they answer, you're in a heap of trouble." If you mistakenly step onto a mound of the "honorees," you'll probably make record time in the festival's road races. You can soothe your pain by sampling the entries in the Strawberry Cookoff. If you'd like to try your calling skills, contact the Ashburn-Turner County Chamber of Commerce, 238 East College Avenue, Ashburn; (229) 567–9696, (800) 471–9696; www.turnerchamber.com.

One Gargantuan Goober
Ashburn

In honor of its status as one of Georgia's most valuable cash crops, Turner Countians put up what's purportedly "The World's Largest Peanut." Standing a regal 20 feet tall, the Big Goober stands proudly alongside I-75 near Ashburn. To see it up close, take exit 82/Highway 107/East Washington Avenue into Ashburn, left on Whittle Circle, and follow the signs to the Peanut and a gazebo, where you can have a picnic. Peanut butter, anyone?

Jay Bird Springs
Chauncey

Jay Bird Springs might make you think, "Nekkid as a . . ." But before you start peeling, bear in mind that southeast Georgia is a loop on the Bible Belt, and a nudist camp would be as likely as a pin-striped coondog. According to local lore, a good many years back a logger who accidentally injured his leg followed a bluejay to a natural spring bubbling from the ground. He bathed his leg in the spring's mineral waters and, lo and behold, was healed. When word got around, people came from everywhere to test the healing waters for themselves. The owner of the land hadn't fallen off a turnip truck—he built a 60-by-100-foot spring-fed swimming pool, and folks still come to heal their weary spirits, if not their injured bodies. To assist the therapy, around the pool there's a water slide and a roller-skating rink, ball fields, picnic grounds, miniature golf, and campgrounds. The pool's at 1221 Jay Bird Springs Road in the small community of Chauncey, on U.S. Highway 341, 4 miles south of Eastman. Phone (229) 868–2728.

Rattlesnakes and Fruitcakes

Claxton

It's just not true what prissy snobs, effete "gourmets," and snotty talk-show hosts say about it. There is most assuredly—thank you very much—more than one fruitcake passed around from household to household, ignominiously used as a doorstop, hockey puck, or third base. The Claxton Bakery Company annually turns out six million pounds of the traditional holiday treat, and many people actually enjoy them, with and without a dousing of strong bourbon or rum. And contrary to popular belief, the pastry that made this southeast Georgia town of 5,000 "The Fruitcake Capital of the World" isn't an old Southern-family recipe. Dale Parker, Claxton Bakery's CEO, says it's an Old World recipe, brought to Claxton in 1910 by Savino Tos, an Italian immigrant who somehow ended up in Claxton and sold his cakes at a local bakery. The bakery was bought after World War II by Parker's dad, Albert, who worked for Tos as a lad. The elder Parker, who died in 1995, took his old boss's recipe and turned it into mass production, which reaches its peak from September to December, when cakes heavy with pineapple,

Please refrain from fruitcake jokes in the municipality of Claxton. The "Fruitcake Capital of the World" annually produces some six million pounds of the holiday treat, which traces its origin to an Italian immigrant.

Old Fashion Claxton Fruit Cake

BAKED IN THE DEEP SOUTH, ACCORDING TO A FAMOUS OLD SOUTHERN RECIPE.

WORLD FAMOUS!

213

Now here's a skill we didn't learn in Home Ec. A herpetologist shows one of the crowned heads of the Claxton Rattlesnake Roundup the art of milking a diamondback, without paying the consequences.

cherries, lemon and orange peel, pecans, and walnuts land on Thanksgiving and Christmas tables around the globe.

If you're here the second weekend of March, your olfactory glands will get mixed signals from the cooking cakes and hissing snakes, which put up a gosh-awful stink when they're kidnapped from their dens and subjected to unspeakable indignities. Ignoring protests from snakes-rights activists, the annual Evans County Rattlesnake Roundup transforms a vigilante hunt for venomous rattlesnakes into a country fair, with marching bands, rock and country wailers, beauty queens, barbecue and funnel cakes, arts and crafts, Shriners, clowns, military drill teams, and grinning politicians.

The roundup began in the late 1960s, when an Evans County teenager was harpooned by an Eastern diamondback rattler while clearing brush on his family farm. He survived, but his near death experience was a call to arms. Today, hundreds of reptile hunters fan around fields and piney woods, bagging sacks full of very put-out vipers. Prizes are given for the biggest, fattest, and most snakes captured by a team—a "champeen" can measure up to 7 feet and weigh in at nearly fifteen pounds, and send a good-size human to glory with a single bite. The critters are milked for their deadly venom, which is used against them as antivenin. The meat (don't they say it tastes like chicken?) is sold to connoisseurs of exotic cuisine. Their skin becomes shoes, boots, belts, hatbands, and handbags. And won't your fashion-conscious friends be pea green when you come home dangling très-chic earrings created from a departed diamondback's rattler string?

The Claxton Bakery, 203 West Main Street, near the center of town (800–841–4211; www.claxtonfruitcake.com), offers free samples Monday through Saturday during its September to December production season. The Claxton-Evans County Chamber of Commerce (912–739–1391; www.claxtonevanschamber.com) can fill you in on the roundup.

THE GNAT LINE

Driving I–75 south of Atlanta on a steaming hot summer day, you innocently get out of your car for a pit stop where I–16 splits off at downtown Macon and bends southeasterly for Metter, Dublin, and Vidalia. Whammo! They're on you like white on rice. They hit you in the face, waging a blitzkrieg on your ears, eyes, and nasal passages. They buzz, they bite, they drive you bazoobies. They zing any exposed flesh and chase you back to your car like Sheriff Jackie Gleason highballing after Burt Reynolds in *Smokey and the Bandit*. Friends, you've crossed the Gnat Line, an insect Maginot Line that separates the state's hilly northern regions from the swampy flatlands. In high-gnat season, normally loquacious natives south of the Gnat Line are more close-mouthed—lest stem-winding yarn become an open invitation for invasion. And all those friendly roadside waves might just be futile flags of surrender. But if you can't beat 'em, invite 'em to a party. The voracious little kamikazes are honored guests at Camilla's Gnat Days the first weekend of May. Contact the Camilla Chamber of Commerce at (229) 336–5255.

Redneck Games

East Dublin

Instead of the same old high jumps, hurdles, decathlons, and marathons, the Redneck Games in East Dublin's Buckeye Park pit competitors in such feats as the armpit serenade (usually won hands-down by pubescent boys, who practice these rude sound effects year-round). Others go head-to-head bobbin' with their teeth for pigs' feet in K-Mart plastic buckets (the record is held by a Milledgeville man, who chomped up eight piggy trotters in an astonishing fifteen seconds). Competition's also keen in the hubcap hurl, watermelon seed spitting, and mud pond diving (judged on your form as you belly flop into an ooey-gooey, soupy-slimy pit of red Georgia clay).

Dublin Radio station WQZY–FM came up with the games in 1996 to deflate some of the hot air from the Summer Olympic Games up the road in Atlanta. Thanks to reams of PR on MTV, *Good Morning America*, and the BBC, and in *Time* and *Sports Illustrated*, the first year's crowd of 500 has mushroomed to more than 15,000. Couples say their wedding vows here. Instead of marching down the aisle to Mendelssohn's same-old "Wedding March," the groom in Confederate gray and his bride clutching a bouquet of Rebel flags are serenaded by the romantic strains of the Bellamy Brothers classic, "Give Me a Redneck Girl." Local officials who first denounced the games as demeaning and degrading now give their blessing to mud-floppers and seed-spitters who green the economy by more than $250,000.

The games are held on Saturday in early July. If you'd like to take part, or just view the madness, take I–16 exit 51/US 441 north to Dublin and U.S. Highway 80 to East Dublin, and then listen for the dulcet tones of the armpit serenade. Admission fee per vehicle. To get an inkling of what you're in for, visit www.redneckgames.tripod.com. For information call (478) 272–4422.

Blue and Gray Together
Fitzgerald

What's this, you say! Streets in a Deep South Georgia town named for Ulysses S. Grant, William T. Sherman (the devil incarnate, as many diehard Southerners still swear), and other Union generals? It's true, and in Fitzgerald (population 8,800) those thoroughfares share equal billing with streets honoring Robert E. Lee, Stonewall Jackson, and fellow Confederate icons. Other arteries are named for trees and flowers native to the North and the South. What's going on here?

In the 1890s Indiana newspaper editor P. H. Fitzgerald, a former Union Army drummer boy, got the notion to build a colony where soldiers from both sides of the conflict could live in harmony. He spearheaded the formation of the American Tribune Soldiers Colony, which purchased 50,000 acres of Georgia piney woods for a brave new town. Nearly 3,000 Yanks and Johnny Rebs from every part of the re–United States moved to the pioneering community, only 10 miles from the spot where Confederate President Jefferson Davis was captured by Union troops. Their descendants have lived in peace and goodwill ever since.

The Blue and Gray Museum, in the former train depot on a street named for Confederate Gen. Joseph E. Johnston, exhibits photos and mementos of the colony's early days, as well as Union and Confederate war relics. It's open from March to October, Monday through Friday 1:00 to 5:00 P.M. Call (229) 426–5033 or visit www.fitzgeraldga.org. Fitzgerald is 28 miles east of I–75 exit 78/ Highway 32/Jefferson Davis Highway.

Ain't Nobody Here but Us Chickens . . .

Fitzgerald

Why do the chickens cross the streets of downtown Fitzgerald with down-right impunity? And how did they get to the city of 10,000 in the first place? It's one of those don't-mess-with-Mother-Nature kinds of stories.

In the 1960s, the Georgia Department of Natural Resources released colorful Burmese junglefowl around the state as game birds to be hunted for sport, like pheasant, quail, and doves. Flocks of the Southeast Asia natives, sporting brilliant orange and yellow plumage and gleaming black tail feathers, were set out on the Ocmulgee River, a few miles from Fitzgerald. They apparently decided they favored city lights over rural tranquility and made their way to town, where they've propagated and prospered ever since.

Alesia Biggers with the Fitzgerald Chamber of Commerce says there are "about a kazillion of them right now," although by most accounts they probably number between 2,000 and 5,000. They've become a tourist curiosity in the city best known for the harmonious relationship between Union and Confederate veterans who settled here after the Civil War. But like the Late Unpleasantness, the chickens are a source of fightin' words. Residents have a love/hate relationship with the wild birds. Some dispense feed to the meandering flocks. They've fostered the Wild Chicken Festival in March, sport T-shirts, coffee mugs, and bumper stickers with "Love Dem Wild Chickens." The disenchanted chase them from their yards and gardens with brooms and a few salty words. The "pros" contend the birds eat insects and other bugs and are a free form of crime prevention, loudly crowing if something disturbs their nightly roosts. "Cons" say they screech at cars that challenge their strolls across city streets, scratch up lawns and flower beds, and leave unhealthy "souvenirs."

In 2005, the city council appointed a committee of two "pros," two "cons," and two council members to puts reins on the free-range population. Options included trapping, feeding them drugged food to make them sterile, and even hiring a chicken catcher, as Key West, Florida, has done. Thus far, Alesia Biggers says, no action has been taken and like 'em or not, the city still harbors its clucking, crowing, unofficial mascots.

Contact the Fitzgerald Convention & Visitors Bureau, 115 South Main Street, Firzgerald; (800) 386–4642; www.fitzgeralddga.org.

Jiminy Crickets!
Glennville

In 1946 Tal Armstrong collected a mess of Australian gray crickets in a Montgomery, Alabama, trash dump and discovered, to his joy, that fish preferred the Down Under natives to the more common wild black crickets. "Granddaddy started off with a hobby, then a small business, and fifty-six years later, we're working our tails off," says Tal's grandson, Jeff Armstrong.

"We've got Armstrong's Cricket Farm in Glennville and another one over in Louisiana. Here in Glennville we usually have around 25 million crickets on hand at most any one time." What on earth would you do with 25 million crickets? "We sell the fool out of 'em," Jeff laughs. "At the Glennville farm, fishermen buy about 70 percent; the rest go to the reptile business, where people feed 'em to lizards, frogs, and snakes. Spiders like 'em, too. In Louisiana it's about 80 percent to pet people for reptiles and 20 percent for fishing." All those crickets make one god-awful racket, but Armstrong says, "One cricket in a room will drive you nuts. When you've got 25 million, it's like an engine going all the time. You don't notice it after a while."

Glennville (population 3,600) is a little short on tourist attractions, so Jeff's mama, who works for the chamber of commerce, sends visitors down to the cricket farm for a tour. "When people show up, we're happy to show 'em around," he says. The farm's on U.S. Highway 301, 306 Gordon Street, near downtown Glennville. Take I–16 exit 116/US 301/25, and keep going south till you hear the sound of a big humming engine. Phone (800) 658–3408. You can order crickets online at www.armstrongcrickets.com.

Harness Racing Festival

Hawkinsville

In a state where pari-mutuel wagering is verboten, Hawkinsville's annual Harness Racing Festival is a rare opportunity to see pedigreed horses do their stuff. On an early-April Saturday and Sunday, several thousand horse fanciers overflow the wooden grandstand and admire the syncopated grace of horses prancing to the commands of jockeys riding behind them in two-wheeled sulkies.

Hawkinsville's Harness Racing Festival gives Georgians the rare opportunity to see top-of-the-line horses go head-to-head, and to place a few discreet bets on their favorites.

Harness horses have been part of Hawkinsville and Pulaski County (population 8,300) since the late nineteenth century. In those days the gentry all had horses for riding and pulling their carriages and buggies. "Betcha my horse can outrun that nag of yours," they'd challenge one another. So, come Sunday afternoon after church, they'd put their respective steeds to the test—with polite wagers on the side, of course. In 1894 Hawkinsville became a stop on the Grand Racing Circuit between Illinois and Florida. The horsemen liked the mild Georgia winters and encouraged the city to build a training facility. The newest complex, built in the 1980s, stables up to 500 horses. They work through the winter months with owners and trainers, who carefully watch for signs of champions with the heart to capture harness racing's equivalent of Thoroughbred racing's Triple Crown.

The Harness Racing Festival is their coming-out party—time to show their stuff before breaking camp and moving north to the big-money harness racing tracks in Illinois, Michigan, Ohio, New Jersey, and Canada. The Harness Racing Festival has the festive air of a county fair. Between races patrons browse booths filled with T-shirts, pottery, paintings, and homemade jams and jellies. They can groove on live country music and stuff themselves with cotton candy, funnel cakes, barbecue, and hot dogs. Although official wagering's illegal, nobody's gonna quibble about gentlemanly wagers between friends.

Hawkinsville is on US 341, 22 miles south of I–75 exit 127/Perry. Call the Hawkinsville-Pulaski County Chamber of Commerce at (478) 783–1717 or visit www.hawkinsville.org.

Jefferson Davis's Last Stand

Irwinville

The end came for Jefferson Davis on the cool, foggy morning of May 10, 1865. Gen. Robert E. Lee had already surrendered at Appomattox, and Davis had dissolved the Confederate Cabinet a week earlier at Washington, Georgia. But the Confederate president still harbored hopes of crossing the Mississippi and fighting on with unconquered Rebel forces in Texas and Louisiana. He and his family and a small military escort were camped in a pine forest near Irwinville; surprised by the Michigan Cavalry's Fourth Regiment, they meekly surrendered. Eager to vilify the detested Davis, the Northern press reported that he was captured disguised in women's clothes (historians say he was wearing a cape in the cool early morning fog). Davis was imprisoned in Virginia but was released after two years and no trial. He died in New Orleans in 1889 and is buried in Richmond, Virginia, his once-capital city.

Jefferson Davis Memorial Historic Site, on the National Register of Historic Places, includes a museum with Civil War weapons and uniforms and an historic marker with a bust of Davis at the place where he was captured. Donations welcome. Call (229) 831–2335. The historic site is 14 miles east of I–75, exit 78.

Miss Liberty
McRae

There's no need to travel all the way to New York to see the Statue of Liberty. Just come on down to McRae and see Telfair County's own version. Standing 32 feet tall—one-twelfth the size of the original in New York Harbor—she's a commanding presence in Liberty Square, at the junction of Highways 23, 280, 441, and 319 in the middle of the town of 3,100. Local craftsmen fashioned her entirely from local wood and unveiled her on July 4, 1986. Her head was carved from a black gum tree, her torch from cypress. A local boat builder wrapped her in a protective fiberglass coating. While you're admiring Lady Liberty, look around at the replica of the Liberty Bell, the U.S. Constitution, and a memorial to Telfair Countians who've died in service to our country.

McRae is at the junction of the above-mentioned highways, 23 miles south of I–16 exit 51/ US 319 and 441. To find out more call (229) 868–6365 or visit www.telfairco.com.

Oasis on I–16
Metter

The 165-mile ride on I–16 between Macon and Savannah is so numbingly monotonous that many drivers liken it to traversing a pine-treed desert. What a blessing to stumble onto Michael Guido Gardens, a lush oasis 2 miles from exit 104 at Metter. Alongside Sower Studios, whence television evangelist Michael Guido, DD, produces his Seed from the Sower broadcasts, "God's Three Acres" are planted with shade trees, flowers, biblical topiaries, and a topiary of Guido himself. Fountains gurgle, waterfalls splash, birds sing, and crickets chirp. A brooklet winds past gazebos and benches and a 24–7 chapel, where motorists can pray for swift, painless passage across I–16. It's open daily, free of charge; during December the gardens are illuminated by a zillion Christmas lights and Nativity scenes. You're also welcome to tour the broadcast studios Monday through Friday and see the Guido sow his telemessage. Phone (912) 685–2222 or visit www.guidogardens.com.

Michael, is that you? A gardener with an artist's touch fashioned this leafy topiary of radio evangelist Michael Guido at Guido Gardens at Metter.

Ride 'Em Gator!

Okefenokee Swamp

What do rangers in Stephen C. Foster State Park, on an island 18 miles inside the Okefenokee National Wildlife Refuge, do for amusement? Why, they joyride a gator, of course. On a boat tour of the mighty swamp a few years ago, interpretive ranger Pete Griffin told us how it's done.

"First thing you need to do," he explained, "is coax an unsuspecting gator alongside your boat, then you roll out of the boat onto his back. Don't worry about his tail slapping you off—his snout's your main concern. Take your thumbs and forefingers and snap the snout shut. As long as you've got it clamped tight, he can't open it again, but if you happen to leave some fingers in there, he can slam that snout down with about 1,000 to 3,000 pounds of pressure per square inch and have your fingers for a snack. It's best to get 'em out of his way. Now that his mouth's closed, open yours and take a big breath, because this gator's going to ride you straight to the bottom. Aim his snout upwards then, and he'll ride you back up to the surface like an elevator. You can steer him right, steer him left, ride him like a pony. What happens when you're ready to get off? Well, that's going to be subject to some serious negotiating between you and Mr. Gator. But whatever you do, you best be quick about it."

Interpretive ranger Pete Griffin was intent on finding a gator to joyride as he piloted tourists through the Okefenokee Swamp in southeast Georgia's Stephen C. Foster State Park, circa 1990. Safe from gators' hungry jaws, Griffin now deciphers mountain nature at Smithgall Woods Conservation Area, near Helen.

To a boatload of snickers, he replied: "I'll remind you that you are in the thick of the Bible Belt, and everything you hear today is gospel."

Stephen C. Foster State Park is off Highway 177, north of Fargo, 18 miles inside the Okefenokee Swamp National Wildlife Refuge. Call (912) 637–5274 or (800) 864–PARK or visit www.gastateparks.org.

Two-in-One Covered Bridge
Twin City

At 100 feet long and 40 feet wide, the Parrish Mill Covered Bridge in George L. Smith State Park isn't Georgia's longest or shortest. What distinguishes it is its grist- and sawmill that have been part of the structure since it was built in 1880. The Georgia Department of Transportation says: "Doors at either end of the mill allow through [pedestrian] traffic, technically qualifying the mill as a covered bridge." So there you have it—officially. A dam on Fifteen Mile Creek provides the power that grinds the corn into cornmeal that's sold to visitors at the park office. Along with his other duties, Park Ranger Tim Almond is the part-time gristmill operator. When the supply runs low, he cranks up the machinery and turns out another batch of Parrish Mill Cornmeal. Local cooks swear by it.

The park also offers nourishment to canoeists and boaters, who thread their way through the 413-acre millpond, studded with bald cypress trees wearing mantles of Spanish moss, and follow 10 miles of water trails. Fishermen flock here, too, with visions of crappie, bream, and catfish sizzling in the frying pan as they keep a wary eye on snatch-and-grab blue herons and white ibises. Hikers share the 11 miles of land trails with gopher tortoises, Georgia's "official" state reptile. Almond says there's a heavy demand for the 1,634-acre park's twenty-five trailer and RV sites and foursome of furnished cottages, especially on weekends.

Crowds are really big for April's Antique Car Show and October's Arts & Crafts Festival. All this water is also popular with you-know-whats, so keep a lookout. The park was named for George L. Smith II, late longtime speaker of the Georgia House of Representatives from Emanuel County. Call (478) 763–2759 or (800) 864–PARK or visit www.gastateparks.org. The park is on Highway 23, 10 miles north of I–16 exit 104.

A bag of freshly ground cornmeal is the reward for visitors who walk the old wooden planks of the Parrish Mill Covered Bridge in George L. Smith State Park, near Twin City, a little town that touts itself as "Twice as Friendly, Twice as Nice."

GETTING OUT OF A GATOR'S GRASP

Oh, Lordy, you've gone and gotten too close to the Okefenokee's chocolate waters and a hungry 'ol gator has jumped out and grabbed you.

Swampers who've been in a similar pickle advise you to keep a cool head and follow these simple steps to extricate yourself:

- If you've been snatched on land, try to get on the gator's back and put pressure on its neck, forcing its head and jaws down to the ground.
- Take a tip from old Western movies, where the cowboy puts a bandana over his horse's eyes to keep it from panicking over a fire or a rattlesnake—get out your hanky or a wad of wet leaves and cover the gator's eyes. That will confuse him and make him less ornery.
- If he's obviously set on having you for brunch, forget the above and use your fists or a stick to poke him in the eyes and snout. While he's crying foul, make a quick getaway. Gators can run faster than a speeding bullet, but they can't climb trees, so find a friendly live oak or cypress and scamper up as high as you can.
- If his jaws clamp around something you'd like to keep (i.e., arms, legs), tap or punch him on the snout. Gators often open their snout when they get a good rap and drop whatever they've gotten hold of, figuring there are easier meals elsewhere.
- If the gator gets you in his jaws, clamp his mouth shut to prevent him from shaking you like a rag doll or rolling over on his back. These instinctive actions really hurt a lot—and you might drown.
- Call 911 ASAP—even if you get away with only a small cut or bruise. Gators' mouths are open sewers of pestilential infection.

Most important, to avoid close encounters of a terminal kind, look before you leap. Don't wade or swim in places gators have staked out. In south Georgia, that could be any creek or swamp. Never feed them—they assume that humans are as tasty as the Twinkies and leftover tuna sandwiches tossed from a boat or dock, so on a hot steamy day, don't dangle your arms and legs over the side of the boat. Gator babies are cute as the dickens, but let 'em be. A youngun's 911 call brings mama on the gallop. Several years ago on Cumberland Island, a novice naturalist and I happened on a gator's hive-shape nest. To my horror the naturalist said, "Oh, I don't see the mother. I'll see if I can call her." I heard the guy's loud, honking sound as I barreled through the underbrush like the cartoon roadrunner. I never saw that naturalist again.

I may look as slow and sluggish as a beached whale, but if you tempt me with Twinkies or Doritos, I'm faster than Seattle Slew down the stretch at Churchill Downs.

The Onion That Could

Vidalia

Agriculturally, it was tantamount to the discovery of gold in the north-east Georgia mountains. But as far as anybody knows, in 1931 when Toombs County farmer Mose Coleman discovered that the onions in his field weren't eye-watering hot but as sweet as a Red Delicious apple, he didn't shout "Eureka!"

At first, sweet onions were a hard sell. The hybrid yellow granex didn't look like a regular onion—it was round on the bottom and flat on the top stem end. People never heard of such, and shied away like they would a polka-dotted coondog. But Coleman was apparently a stubborn cuss. To get people to try 'em, he'd sell a fifty-pound bag for $3.50. That was a heap of onions for Depression-era change. (Today, you'll get about a five-pound sack for that same amount.) Pretty soon, housewives around Vidalia started using them. "Hey, I can chop these up and not get all teary-eyed!" they told their friends, who told theirs. Other farmers saw what was happening, figured Coleman had stumbled onto a gold mine and planted their fields with the sweet, mild-tasting onions. In the 1940s the state of Georgia put up a farmers' market in Vidalia conveniently situated at the junction of a mess of busy highways, where tourists passed on their way to Florida and the Georgia coast. They bought bagsful and spread the message about "those Vidalia onions" far and wide. An unsung somebody gave them their famous name and before you knew it, Vidalia Sweet Onions were on the shelves of Piggly Wiggly and A&P stores. By the mid-1970s, more than 600 acres were planted. Those acres kept increasing geometrically—and so did the demand. By the 1980s Vidalias were in markets from Portland, Maine, to Portland, Oregon, and across the seas in Europe and Japan. Today, about 275 growers cultivate Vidalias on more than 10,000 acres.

A lot of folks wanted to get in on the good thing—forgers in Alabama, Mississippi, southwest Georgia, and other far-off places started bagging up hot onions and labeling them Vidalias. Something had to be done. In 1986 the Georgia legislature gave the Vidalia onion legal status and defined a twenty-county area of southeast Georgia as its official production area. In 1990 the Vidalia onion was declared Georgia's "Official State Vegetable." What makes them so sweet is a unique combination of sandy, loamy soil and mild climate conditions. Temperatures in the production area average in the mid-50s in winter and mid-70s in spring, with an average rainfall of 3½ inches during the growing season. The onions mature and are harvested from late April through mid-June. Their delicate nature requires that they be harvested by hand, thoroughly dried, and treated gently during grading and packaging. Recent technological advances in controlled-atmosphere storage have extended the marketing season well past the summer months. The only thing sweeter than biting into a Vidalia is the $150-million blessing it annually showers on the state's economy. You can eat 'em like an apple or try 'em these easy ways:

Honey Baked Onions

Preheat oven to 325 degrees.
4 large Vidalia Sweet Onions, peeled and trimmed
In a separate bowl mix:
1½ cups tomato juice
1½ cups water
6 teaspoons melted butter
6 teaspoons honey

Cut the onions in half and place them in a buttered baking dish, flat sides up. Pour the sauce over the onions. Bake at 325 degrees for one hour, or until soft. Serves about 8.

Vidalia Onion Salad

4 medium Vidalia Sweet Onions, sliced thin
   and separated into rings
½ cup sugar
¼ cup wine vinegar
1 cup water
1½ tablespoons mayonnaise
1½ teaspoons celery seed
Green or red leaf lettuce
Pimientos or ripe olives for garnish

Combine sugar, vinegar, and water. Stir until the sugar dissolves. Soak onion rings in the solution at least 2 hours in the refrigerator. Drain the rings. Stir in the mayonnaise and celery seeds. Serve on lettuce leaves. Garnish with pimiento strips and/or olive slices.

Needless to say, don't try these recipes with ordinary onions. The results will be disastrous. These and many other terrific dishes with Vidalias are served at May festivals in Vidalia and neighboring Glennville. To learn all about it, and maybe take a farm tour, contact the Vidalia Tourism Council; (912) 538–8687; www.vidaliaga.com. Vidalia is on US 280, 16 miles south of I–16 exit 84/Highway 297.

The Mummified Dog

Waycross

Some time back, a four-year-old brown-and-white hound chased a rabbit or squirrel into a hollow chestnut oak tree in northwest Georgia's Haralson County. The prey escaped. The hound did not. Years later, when loggers were cutting the tree into 7-foot pulpwood lengths, they found the doomed doggie still inside, almost perfectly preserved, a terrified howl frozen on his face. He was lodged 20 feet up in the tree, a few tantalizing feet short of the exit hole; a chimney effect in the hollow tree created upward drafts of air, preventing the deceased's scent from attracting insects and other predators. The tree also provided a relatively dry environment, and its tannic acid hardened the dog's skin and mummified him like old King Tut. Today he's at Southern Forest World Museum, 1440 North Augusta Avenue in Waycross; (912) 285–4056.

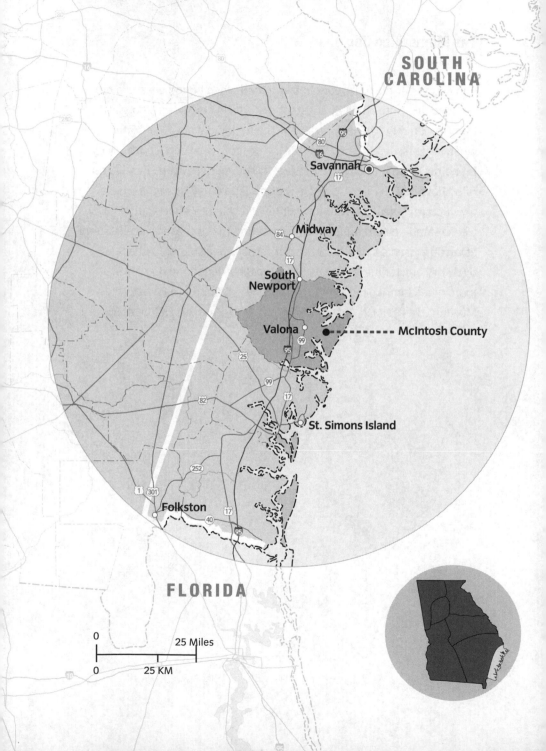

COASTAL GEORGIA

SOUTH
CAROLINA

Savannah

Midway

South
Newport

Valona ●----------- McIntosh County

St. Simons Island

Folkston

FLORIDA

0
25 Miles

0
25 KM

COASTAL GEORGIA

Ghosts and tales of ghosts are as thick as the Spanish moss that hangs over the colonial towns and sun-kissed isles of Georgia's 120-mile Cote d'Azur. The coast's flagship, Savannah, has a mess of spirits and other curiosities. Bring a little something for *Midnight in the Garden of Good and Evil* victim Danny Hansford, still partying it up in the port city's Bonaventure Cemetery. Raise a beaker of Chatham Artillery Punch to Forrest Gump, and look for Little Gracie in the cafeteria line at Piccadilly. Down the coast, beware of St. Simons Island's tree spirits, the colonial spooks that come out at night in vanished Sunbury, and the Revolutionary War heroes that march around Midway Churchyard. Kick back with wild nature at Melon Bluff's 10,000 acres of woodlands and salt marshes, or dig into fresh-caught shrimp and oysters. Weary and depressed? Consult an unorthodox therapist named Northern Spy; he may mo-o-ove you back to health.

Waitin' for the Train(s)

Folkston

For most of us, waiting for a freight train to pass is one of life's small downers. We fume, fuss, and fret that the darn thing will never end. And if it temporarily stalls, forget it! For folks in Folkston, freights are high points of the day. Alerted by the scratchy voice of an unseen dispatcher, avid rail junkies go into high gear. They aim their video cameras and speculate excitedly about what type of train will soon be rumbling through "The Folkston Funnel."

Pretty soon, the jangling alarm on a nearby crossing gate breaks the solitude of a quiet weekday morning. Moments later, an ear-shattering horn announces the arrival of a mammoth blue, yellow, and silver CSX engine pulling a seemingly endless line of cars laden with lumber, coal, chemicals, autos, agriculture, whatever.

It's show time in Folkston, a town of 2,500 on the Georgia-Florida border, 40 miles northwest of Jacksonville.

Folkston's tracks aren't your everyday tracks. Two major CSX lines converging on the north side of town funnel some forty to seventy trains through town every day of the week, which means every freight train bound between Florida and the Eastern half of the United States must pass through Folkston. Added to the mix are three daily Amtrak passenger trains, whose riders are surprised by waving, cheering well-wishers.

Thus, the name "Folkston Funnel."

In 2001, townsfolk looking for a way to harvest tourist dollars decided all those trains might lure some of the visitors who come to nearby Okefenokee Swamp National Wildlife Refuge.

"I don't think we'll ever be able to compete with the swamp and all those gators," says Marvin "Cookie" Williams, the Folkston Funnel's biggest champion, "but it's amazing the number of people who come here to watch the trains."

Williams and fellow and lady enthusiasts brought Folkston Mayor Dixie McGurn on board, and she, in turn talked the state of Georgia into a $30,000 grant to build a wooden platform a safe distance from the tracks.

Modeled after a Lionel model train platform, Folkston's has a roof, a ceiling fan, comfortable chairs, picnic tables, a grill, and restrooms. A scanner picks up radio chatter between engineers and control towers. For those who can't get enough trains by day, floodlights illuminate the tracks after dark.

To get the word out, the city advertises in train magazines. Brochures at state welcome centers hawk the attraction. Folkston motels offer discounts to rail fans, and restaurants feature train-themed entrees.

On most any given day, fans from several different states and tourists from as far away as Britain and Australia show up to videotape the trains, talk train talk, and just admire the behemoths as they roll though the Funnel. Phone (912) 496–2536 or visit www.folkston.com.

Praying for Sheetrock

McIntosh County

Melissa Fay Greene took the title of her 1991 best-selling nonfiction book, *Praying for Sheetrock*, from a curious chapter in McIntosh County history. Until I–95 was built in the 1970s, Florida-bound northerners and cargo-bearing trucks were funneled through coastal Georgia on US 17. South of Savannah, the gullible snowbirds were plucked by shell games and speed traps sanctioned by McIntosh County Sheriff Tom Poppell. The high sheriff used the antiquated highway as kings of yore used their patronage. When the eighteen-wheelers high-balling the treacherous, fogbound highway inevitably overturned, Sheriff Poppell shrewdly allowed his poverty-strapped subjects to reap the windfall of shoes, frozen food, building materials, and other precious commodities. In repayment, they forgave his corruption and returned him to office for thirty-one years.

Fanny Palmer, an African-American shrimp peeler, didn't want sneakers or TV dinners. She prayed for Sheetrock to keep the elements and swamp critters from her sharecropper cabin. She prayed so earnestly that one night two trucks carrying Sheetrock shipments to builders up north collided and overturned, showering the highway with the answer to Fanny Palmer's supplications, with a gracious plenty left over for her neighbors. "Ain't God a good God?" she marveled. *Praying for Sheetrock*, which chronicles the political and social awakening of McIntosh County's African-American community, and the downfall of one of Georgia's last political dynasties, was published by Addison-Wesley Publishing. Greene also is the author of *The Temple Bombing*, about the 1960s attack on an Atlanta synagogue, and *Last Man Out*, about a 1950s Nova Scotia mine disaster with a bizarre Coastal Georgia twist.

Midway Church
Midway

Midway Congregational Church rises from the mossy live-oak groves like a New England meeting house that's come to the Georgia coast for the winter. In a sense it did. The white clapboard church, with its gabled roof and square belfry, straight-backed pews, high pulpit, and slave gallery, is virtually all that's left of the town of Midway, founded by Massachusetts Puritans in 1754. But some interesting men walked through its front door. In its prime the church's parishioners included two of Georgia's three signers of the Declaration of Independence. Connecticut-born physician Dr. Lyman Hall later became Georgia's governor and, old Yalie that he was, laid the groundwork for the state university system. Less than a year after penning his "John Hancock" on the Declaration,

English-born Button Gwinnett was killed in a pistol duel with a political rival (he was only forty-five, didn't leave too many documents behind, and his signature is now worth a fortune). The fathers of Oliver Wendell Holmes and Samuel F. B. Morse served as pastors. Revolutionary War heroes Gen. James Screven and Gen. Daniel Stewart (Theodore Roosevelt's great-grandfather) lie under the lichen-covered stones in the churchyard. During the Union Army's occupation of Liberty County in the winter of 1864, the church escaped the fires that destroyed virtually every other building because the soldiers used it to stable their horses. The last official service was conducted in 1865, but the church remains a popular place for weddings and events that don't require electricity or other contemporary niceties.

Three Georgia signers of the Declaration of Independence were parishioners at Midway Church in Liberty County. Theodore Roosevelt's great grandfather, a Revolutionary War hero, is buried in the churchyard.

Pick up the big iron church key at the Gulf station across the road or the adjacent Midway Museum, an eighteenth-century raised cottage with furniture and other memorabilia from colonial times to the Civil War. The docent will dip a finger in vinegar and play you an eerie tune on a set of wine glasses. Take Interstate 95 exit 76/Highway 38/US 84 and go west 4 miles to US 17. Admission fee. Call (912) 884–5837.

Northern Spy, Family Pet
Midway

"Northern Spy looks like an ox, but he's really a philosopher," observed Don Devendorf, one of the owners of Melon Bluff, a 10,000-acre nature preserve and bed-and-breakfast on the coast near Midway. "People come here from Atlanta and other big cities, all tensed up and stressed out, and after talking with Spy for a few minutes, they unwind and start enjoying themselves. After a day or so, we can't get them out of here."

A short-horn cross male, Spy was named for the Northern Spy apples he enjoyed at his former home at Old Sturbridge Village, Massachusetts. Don and Laura Devendorf and their daughter, Meredith, adopted the big ox while Meredith was a student at Amherst College. They wanted a signature animal for their barnyard at Melon Bluff, and Spy was amenable to the change in scenery and warmer climate. He's adapted beautifully but still occasionally moos with a New Englandy accent. Spy doesn't get many Northern Spys in southern Georgia, but he hasn't forgotten the taste of his favorite fruit. "When the cooks are making apple pancakes and apple turnovers, he gets the peelings and cores," says Don. "Sometimes our guests go out to the local markets and bring apples back for him."

Not that he's finicky. He seems just as happy with handfuls of Spanish moss pulled from the trees, crunchy chiggers and all, and when a large old pine tree fell in his pasture while I was there, he loped over and helped himself to the free foliage buffet. Along with his duties as resident therapist, Spy is also a stand-in for the family dog the Devendorfs are reluctant to keep.

"He thinks he's a golden retriever," Meredith says, "a 2,500-pound golden retriever. He loves to be petted and brushed, and sometimes he'll startle our guests by running up to them, wanting to play. That can be pretty unnerving, especially if you're a woman in a pencil dress and high heels."

Spy doesn't have a mate, but he gets along just fine with the goats that share his barnyard. When his picture appeared in *Oglethorpe's Dream: A Picture of Georgia,* a coffee-table book by Georgia Division of Tourism photographer Diane Kirkland, Spy got a personal copy, autographed by Gov. Roy Barnes. He's not saying what he sent the governor in return.

Northern Spy, a philosopher and short-horn ox, snacks on Spanish moss at Melon Bluff Plantation while he waits for the main course of his favorite namesake apples.

Along with Spy's soothing words, Melon Bluff's allures include miles and miles of forested hiking trails; bird-watching for endangered wood storks, painted buntings, and 350 other species; and kayaking in what the Devendorfs believe is the last unpolluted estuary on the entire U.S. eastern seaboard. Don Devendorf passed away after the first edition of *Georgia Curiosities* was published. Laura, Meredith, and Spy uphold the family tradition of conservation and hospitality. Melon Bluff is 3 miles from I–95 and 30 miles south of Savannah. Phone toll-free (888) 246–8188 or visit www.melonbluff.com.

Seabrook Village

Midway

The Union Army's "scorched earth" devastation of Liberty County was so thorough that it deprived even freed slaves of a means to survive. Faced with starvation, they formed a closely knit African-American community called Seabrook Village. Without government assistance, they built homes, churches, and a one-room schoolhouse; planted rice, corn, and other crops; ground cane into syrup; and used their ingenuity to make it through.

The community survived, mostly intact, until the 1930s, when families moved away and the simple homes and buildings began falling to ruins. Since the early 1990s a biracial group of Liberty Countians has been restoring Seabrook Village as a unique African-American living history museum. A guided tour is the best way to hear the message the village's old walls tell. Tours begins at the one-room wooden schoolhouse, built in 1875 and active until 1951. One of the stops on the tour is Seabrook director Florence Roberts's grandfather's uninsulated pine-plank house, built in 1891, where he lived until 1980, when he died at

Florence Roberts cranks the outdoor pump that once provided water to her grandparents and other residents of Seabrook Village, a post–Civil War African-American community that thrived until the 1930s. Many of the village's homes and other structures have been restored and opened to visitors.

age ninety-five. His old featherbed, shaving gear, a few handmade pieces of furniture, and clothes are still there.

"When my grandfather was away for a time, his children put in electricity," Roberts explains. "When he got back, he had them take it out. He said he was too old for modern conveniences." Nearby, Roberts's aunt's house had a spare room for the village's schoolteacher, usually a visiting northerner, and such luxuries as a peanut roaster made from an old Singer sewing machine and photographs artfully framed in wooden matchsticks.

Seabrook Village is 4.5 miles east of I–95 exit 76/Midway and 35 miles south of Savannah. For information phone (912) 884–7008.

SUNDOWN ON SUNBURY

If it hadn't been for the American Revolution and a few other unfortunate happenstances, tourists might be trooping through the picturesque squares of Sunbury's national historic district, not Savannah's. Alas, the Revolution happened, and no trace can now be found of this port city, which flowered and died between 1747 and 1783. Established as a cotton, lumber, and rice shipping port, by 1758 Sunbury was a prosperous little beehive, with eighty dwellings, a customs house, taverns, merchant stores, and other enterprises on a grid of public square, just like Savannah, 30 miles up the coast. Two of Georgia's Declaration of Independence signers—Button Gwinnett and Lyman Hall—lived in the town. (The third signer, George Walton, was held prisoner in the local lockup after the British captured the town in 1778.)

When Georgia joined the Revolution against King George, Fort Morris was built to guard Sunbury from invasion. In November 1778 a British expedition moved on Sunbury and the fort by land and sea. When the British commander demanded surrender, American Col. John McIntosh shot back: "We, sir, are fighting the battle of America. As to surrendering the fort, receive this laconic reply: Come and take it!" The message was as inspiring to Colonel Lewis's troops as the terse "Nuts!" that World War II Brigadier Gen. Anthony McAuliffe hurled at Germans who demanded his surrender at Bastogne during the Battle of the Bulge. It worked—for a while. The British withdrew but returned a month later with a bigger force, in no mood to be bluffed. They bombarded Fort Morris into submission, and Sunbury became a military garrison holding captured American officers.

When the Revolution ended with the 1783 Treaty of Paris, Sunbury and the fort were in ruins. The remaining residents left, and the town dissolved into a ghost town. Today the site is covered with trees and dense foliage. At the Fort Morris State Historic Site (2559 Fort Morris Road, 7 miles west of I–95 exit 76/Highway 38; 912–884–5999 or 800–864–PARK; www.gastateparks.org), a museum and film in the visitor center tell the story of the lost town and the fortress. A marked trail takes you around the fort's earthworks and along the marshes and Medway River to Sunbury's site. A nearby burial grounds, opened in 1758, is the only physical reminder of the town.

Tree Spirits
St. Simons Island

If you're driving down the tree-canopied roads on St. Simons Island, admiring the beauty of the regal old live oaks in their gray-green mantillas of Spanish moss, and suddenly you get a peculiar feeling that the trees are looking back at you—you're not crazy. St. Simons has plenty of ghosts, but the faces peering at you between two huge branches or the stub of a long-vanished branch are real. Local artists carved the weathered faces of the "Tree Spirits" to immortalize the countless seamen who lost their lives on sailing ships made from St. Simons' mighty oaks. The sorrowful, grieving faces seem to reflect the melancholy spirit of the trees themselves. Look for them on Demere Road at Skylane Drive; Demere Road at the Coastal Center for the Arts; Mallery Street in the Village commercial area; Redfern Village, off Frederica Road; and 3305 Frederica Road. For more information contact the Brunswick and Golden Isles Convention & Visitors Bureau; (800) 933–2627; www.bgivb.com.

Bonaventure Cemetery

Savannah

Fans following the trail of *Midnight in the Garden of Good and Evil* (aka "The Book") ultimately wind up their Savannah pilgrimage in Bonaventure Cemetery. It was, after all, here that the narrator of John Berendt's nonfiction best-seller sipped martinis among the dripping Spanish moss and grandiose tombs as he was indoctrinated into the Byzantine world of Savannah society.

Before trekking all the way out here, though, book fans should know that the *Bird Girl* statue on the book's cover isn't here anymore. So many fans wanted to touch her—and take her—that she was brought for safekeeping to the Telfair Museum, downtown. Also, Jim Williams, the book's protagonist, isn't buried in Bonaventure or anywhere else in Savannah. He's in his family's plot near the tiny Middle Georgia town of Gordon, where he grew up and escaped from. However, Danny Hansford, the "wild thang" Williams shot to death, is under a flat marker in the Greenwich section's Section 8, Area G, Plot 58. Danny's sympathizers leave plastic flowers, cig butts, booze bottles, and little plastic sports cars, in case he ever figures a way out.

Non-Book notables resting among the garden's azaleas, camellias, and giant moss-draped live oaks include Pulitzer Prize–winning poet Conrad Aiken, who thoughtfully marked his grave with a marble bench etched with his verse. In the wee hours, does he compare notes with Savannah's beloved lyricist, Johnny Mercer ("Moon River," "Moonlight in Vermont," "Ac-cent-tchu-ate the Positive," and more)?

Bonaventure Cemetery is at 330 Bonaventure Road. Call (912) 651–6843. It's open daily from sunrise to sunset.

Maybe someday Danny Hansford will crank up the little plastic sports car left on his grave at Savannah's Bonaventure Cemetery and drive up to settle the score with his erstwhile friend, Jim Williams, in rural Wilkinson County.

Ghosts of Savannah
Savannah

Ghost watchers declare this seaport is the most haunted city in North America. Revolutionary foot soldiers, Civil War Yanks and Rebs, pirates, old sea dogs, yellow fever victims, and done-wrong lovers rattle the azalea and camellia bushes in gardens and public squares. Scratch a vintage house in the historic district and an apparition is apt to drift out of the woodwork and say "boo!" Like their living counterparts, Savannah's spooks crave the good life—they often show up at restaurants, taverns, and historic inns: "Little Gracie," age six when she died of pneumonia in the 1890s, comes in from Bonaventure Cemetery to check out the baked chicken and congealed salads at a downtown cafeteria.

While you're dining at The Olde Pink House, a gentleman dressed in eighteenth-century finery and powdered wig might drop by your table to ask about the crispy scored flounder with apricot and leek sauce. Tell him it's mighty tasty, then call Ghostbusters. James Habersham passed on more than two centuries ago, but the old bon vivant still comes around from time to time to see how his old place is doing. Another fine establishment, built in the 1750s as a crash pad for sailors and cutthroats, the old wooden boards of the Pirates House restaurant creak with the tread of bygone sea dogs. In a "death imitates art" scenario, one of the walking wraiths might be fictional Captain Flint, who died in an upstairs room in Robert Louis Stevenson's *Treasure Island*. Staff at the Marshall House hotel (built in 1850) swear they've seen a sad-faced young girl in a nineteenth-century white frock walking the fourth-floor corridor. They believe she's lost, looking for her mama and papa. Gentlemen guests at the 17 Hundred 90 Inn awaken to find an invisible female form in their bed. Not to worry, they're told, it's just Annie Powers, still looking for the sailor who sailed away when Thomas Jefferson was president. A yellow tabby cat plays hide-and-seek with staff and visitors at the Davenport House museum. Another phantom kitty chases ghostly mice on the upstairs steps at the Ballastone Inn.

If you'd like to "meet" some of the city's bygone personalities, don't call Ghostbusters, call "Ghost Talk, Ghost Walk" (800–563–3896) or Old Town Trolley's Ghosts and Gravestones (912–233–0083, www.ghosts andgravestones.com).

Apparently not even death by pneumonia more than a century ago can deter "Little Gracie" from nocturnal visits to a downtown Savannah cafeteria. Gracie and other spirits still cherish the port city's love of fine cuisine.

Savannah's First Scandal
Savannah

The founder of Methodism had Savannah's tongues wagging some 250 years before Jim Williams shot Danny Hansford and set off the scandal immortalized in *Midnight in the Garden of Good and Evil.*

John Duncan, book dealer and raconteur extraordinaire, tells the parson's tale with a Chaucerian twinkle:

"John Wesley came to Savannah in the 1730s to minister to the Indians, but he became pastor of Christ Anglican Church. His undoing was falling in love with Hard-Hearted Hannah, the vamp of early eighteenth-century Savannah. It was a classic May-December romance. He was thirty-six, Sophia Hopkey was eighteen. They'd walk hand-in-hand in the moonlight and read poetry together, and he taught her the French tongue, but when he asked her to marry him, she dropped him like a hot potato and married somebody else. Soon after the marriage, when Sophia and her new husband came to Sunday services at Christ Church, Wesley refused to give his former lady friend communion. Sophia's in-laws sued Wesley for defamation of character. He was indicted, but never came to trial. It was Savannah's first big public scandal, of which we've had many ever since."

Duncan has other tales to tell at V&J Duncan Antique Maps & Prints, 12 East Taylor Street; (912) 232–0338.

"Mama Always Said . . ."
Savannah

In the Oscar-winning film *Forrest Gump,* Forrest (Tom Hanks) reduced a succession of Savannahians to sympathetic tears with tales he told while sitting on a bus stop bench in Chippewa Square. The bench was a fiberglass movie prop, and when the film was wrapped, dogmatic historians insisted the faker be moved from beneath founding father James Edward Oglethorpe's bronze likeness. Today the bench where Gump sat his rump is parked in the Savannah History Museum, adjoining the Savannah Visitors Center, 303 Martin Luther King Jr. Boulevard; (912) 238–1779. Admission fee.

Forrest Gump Bench

Seated on a bus stop bench, Tom Hanks, as "Forrest Gump," drew buckets of tears from sympathetic Savannahians. When the film was wrapped, the fiberglass movie prop bench was moved from Chippewa Square to the Savannah History Museum.

Chatham Artillery Punch

Savannah

Founded in 1786 as Georgia's oldest military organization, the Chatham Artillery fortified themselves for cotillions and other battlefronts by quaffing a sweet-tasting, but potentially lethal, concoction named in their honor. Its origins are unrecorded—it's believed that genteel ladies made the first mild batches and that over the years Artillery officers added their own firepower. On a 1791 visit to Savannah, where he was saluted by the twenty-six firings of the Artillery's fieldpieces, George Washington found the punch so tasty that he donated the "Washington Guns" captured from the British at Yorktown in 1781. They're stationed on Factors Walk, still on guard for Redcoats. Here's the recipe, but caveat emptor: One helping will make you happy, two will make you crazy. I once saw a very dignified lady in her seventies, starting on her third glass, light up a foul-smelling cigar, pinch the rear of a waiter who could've been her grandson, and pass the astonished lad her hotel key.

Chatham Artillery Punch

1 quart gin

1½ gallons Catawba wine

½ pint Benedictine

1½ quarts rye whiskey

2½ pounds brown sugar

1½ quarts lemon juice

½ gallon rum

1 quart brandy

2 quarts maraschino cherries

1½ gallons strong tea

1½ quarts orange juice

Mix 36 to 48 hours before serving. At serving time add one case of champagne and the brass buttons from a Confederate officer's uniform.

KUDZU, FROM ONE END OF GEORGIA T'OTHER

It's Supervine! Faster than a speeding bullet! Stops speeding locomotives! Leaps tall buildings in a single bound! Kudzu shrouds the shrubbery in my suburban Atlanta backyard. It hammerlocks trees from the Blue Ridge Mountains' hardwood forests to the live oaks down in Pogoland's Okefenokee Swamp. Slick green leaves the size of dinner platters, with roots tipping nature's scales at nigh-on 400 pounds, take over vacant lots from Atlanta to Zebulon. Vines as cunning as cobras scale fences and utility poles, shorting electrical power, and burying billboards, barns, abandoned houses, stalled cars, and idle tractors. Stand too long in one place in spring and summer, when vines can grow a foot a day, and it'll have you in a sleeper hold faster than you can say WWE.

Kudzu is a part of our landscape; it's entwined in our folklore, our Southern gothic psyche. It's the butt of cynical jokes ("How do you plant kudzu? Just drop the seeds and run like a scalded polecat."), and fodder for plays, poems, songs, cartoons, books, and a litany of nicknames: "The Weed That Ate the South," "The Green Scourge," "The Un-divine Vine," and "The Dracula Plant" (like the Count, it feigns death in winter and returns in spring with a deadly vengeance).

So, to what do we owe the honor?

By all accounts, credit (blame) goes to the Japanese, who brought it over as an ornamental vine to shade their pavilion at the 1876 Philadelphia Centennial Exposition. Watching it grow before wondering eyes was as big an attraction as the exposition's electric lights, telephones, and other man-made marvels. Accustomed to

CONTINUED

Southeast Asia's tropical climate, *pueraria lobata* found a happy home in the hot, humid land below the Mason-Dixon line. As a porch and arbor vine, it provided welcome shade and a delightful scent when its purple flowers bloomed.

Pretty soon, everybody had to have some, and mail order catalogs couldn't fill the orders fast enough. During the Dust Bowl days of the Great Depression, the U.S. Department of Agriculture paid farmers to plant kudzu on their land to help control soil erosion. (Before the USDA came to its senses in the 1940s and realized the stuff was all giddyup and no whoa, Dixie was implanted with more than 100,000 vines.)

It had so many uses, no wonder folks called it "the miracle plant."

No such thing as a free lunch? Try telling that to cattle, hogs, chickens, and sheep that couldn't get enough of the stuff. Humans—mainly "Mikeys" who'd eat anything that didn't sink fangs into them first—also acquired a taste for it. After all, it's a member of the *Leguminosae* plant family, an Asian cousin of the South's beloved black-eye pea (which blended with white rice, ham hock, and onions yields hoppin' john, an ambrosia of Southern gastronomy). With a goodly chunk of fatback or streak-o-lean, kudzu's jade leaves could be boiled for hours and set before a hungry mob like turnip and collard greens. Dredged in egg and flour or cornmeal, it fried up as crunchy and tasty as okra. Home economists developed jams, jellies, soap, and candy from the flowers and noodles, paper, and herbal medicines from the starchy roots. If that gets your appetite to barking, here's a traditional recipe to quiet that puppy down:

Deep Fried Kudzu

Pick kudzu leaves no more than 3 inches in diameter from a patch that's away from places sprayed with herbicides and pesticides. Wash thoroughly and dry on paper towels before frying.

Make a batter of:
1 cup flour
1 beaten egg
½ cup milk
Salt and pepper to taste

Heat 1 cup oil in skillet until a drop of batter browns quickly. Dip each kudzu leaf into the batter and drop into the oil. Fry until the crust is golden brown. Drain on paper towels and serve warm. A few drops of Tabasco sauce give it an extra zingy bite. Then again, except for peach pie and divinity fudge, Tabasco improves the taste of just about everything.

As it creeps north of the Mason-Dixon line, the green monster is acquiring a new handle: "The Confederacy's Revenge." Look out, Gettysburg, here it comes!

DASHING THROUGH THE SQUARES

James Lord Pierpont must have been homesick for his native New England when he wrote the ubiquitous Christmas song "Jingle Bells" in Savannah in 1857. Dashing through the subtropical port city's snowless squares in a one-horse open sleigh would likely have earned him more bumps and bruises than nostalgic holiday cheer. Pierpont was born in Boston in 1822, and his family tree branched all the way back to Charlemagne and William the Conqueror. His father was the grandfather of financial potentate John Pierpont Morgan. James's genes were apparently salted with his ancestors' adventurous spirit. He ran off to sea when he was fourteen and later went West with the gold-seeking 49ers. He disembarked in Savannah in 1852 and played the organ at the Unitarian church, where his brother was pastor. In 1857 he married the daughter of Savannah's Civil War mayor and, with visions of his birthplace's snowy hills and dales dancing in his head, gave the world the tune played ad nauseam during the Nativity holidays. His musical talent also produced "Ring the Bell, Fanny" and other sadly forgotten minstrel songs and ballads. He fought for the Confederacy, died in Florida in 1893, and is buried in Savannah's Laurel Grove Cemetery. A century after his passing, a historical marker was installed in Troup Square, in front of the church where he was organist when "Jingle Bells" jangled his imagination.

"JINGLE BELLS"

James L. Pierpont (1822-1893), composer of "Jingle Bells", served as music director of this church in the 1850s when it was a Unitarian Church located on Oglethorpe Square. Son of the noted Boston reformer, Rev. John Pierpont, he was the brother of Rev. John Pierpont, Jr., minister of this church, and uncle of financier John Pierpont Morgan. He married Eliza Jane Purse, daughter of Savannah mayor Thomas Purse, and served with a Confederate cavalry regiment. He is buried in Laurel Grove Cemetery. A prolific song-writer, his best known "Jingle Bells" is world famous.

Savannah's Miss Daisy
Savannah

Juliette Gordon Low, founder of the Girl Scouts of America in 1912, was creative in more ways than one. "Daisy" Low, as friends and family called her, was a painter and sculptor with a flair for the dramatic and eccentric. On a visit to England, she went trout fishing, dressed in a formal ball gown, with Rudyard Kipling. She adorned her hats with real fruit and vegetables, drove on the right side of the road in England, and on the left side in America.

Juliette may have inherited her penchant for drama from her maternal side. At the age of six, her great-grandmother was kidnapped by Iroquois and held for four years before finally being returned to her family. Juliette's mother literally knocked her future husband off his feet when she slid down a banister and sent him flying, a skill she didn't forget. When she was eighty-one, Juliette's bedridden mother overheard her children in a downstairs parlor making plans for her funeral. Her doctor had forbidden her to use the stairs, so the children were astonished when she appeared in the parlor. "How did you get down?" they asked. "I slid down the banister, of course," she replied.

Juliette claimed that a severe loss of hearing at an early age was actually an advantage. She had such a hard time hearing that she talked all the time and never allowed herself to hear the word "no." You can learn more about Daisy and her family at the Juliette Gordon Low National Girl Scout Center, Bull Street and Oglethorpe Avenue, in downtown Savannah; (912) 233–4501. Admission fee.

Much Ado about Bamboo
Savannah

Quick, now, where do you imagine the world's largest collection of bamboo varieties is on display? If you guessed China, Southeast Asia, or the South Pacific, you're off by many thousands of miles. With 140 varieties flourishing on forty-six acres, the Bamboo Farm and Coastal Gardens, on US 17, 10 miles south of Savannah, takes the prize.

It began in 1890, when Mrs. H. B. Miller planted three bamboo canes in her garden. By 1915, Mrs. Miller's little trio had grown to Herculean proportions, covering more than an acre of the Miller farm with tall, stout stalks. Word of the mighty grove reached the ears of Dr. David Fairchild, head of the U.S. Department of Agriculture's Seed and Plant Introduction Section, who envisioned the farm as an ideal place for a government plant introduction station. If fertile soil, warm, sunny climate, and ample moisture suited the bamboo so well, who knew what else would grow!

Dr. Fairchild shared his idea with Barbour Lathrop, an amateur botanist and plant exploration specialist from Chicago. He was so enthusiastic he bought the farm and resold it to the Agriculture Department for one dollar. With uncharacteristic government speed, the farm became a working USDA Plant Introduction Station, headed by Dr. Fairchild. Barbour Lathrop and other botanists brought bamboo types and other plants from all over the world to test their compatibility with coastal Georgia.

Hundreds of experiments took place. Lakes and ponds were dug to test water chestnuts as an American product. The Hertz Foundation experimented with bamboo to make paper. Goldenrod and dog fennel were tested as substitutes for rubber trees. During the Vietnam War, bamboo did its patriotic duty as material for mock villages to train soldiers at Fort Benning, Georgia. The USDA closed the station in 1978, but four years later the property was deeded to the University of Georgia as a research and education center.

UGA added numerous tree and shrub species including palms, black walnut, crape myrtle, holly, magnolia, Chinese elm, fruit and nut trees, herbs, and lawn grasses. Fields of succulent strawberries flourish in summer. Ducks skim on stocked fishing ponds.

The Bamboo Farm is open to researchers and the general public, free of charge. A Chinese-style museum displays bamboo artifacts. The Friends of the Coastal Gardens, a support group, hosts a number of annual events. Hundreds of coastal residents come out for strawberry picking in spring and supper in the strawberry patch, a "catch 'em and eat 'em" fish fry in summer and wild game dinners in winter. A pavilion built by the Friends hosts weddings, family reunions, gardening classes, and conferences.

Many people come to escape coastal heat and humidity under the shade of the trees and bamboo species that can tower 30 to 70 feet tall and several inches around. For information contact the Bamboo Farm and Coastal Gardens, 2 Canebrake Road, Savannah; (912) 921–5460; www.ces.uga.edu.

America's Smallest Church?
South Newport

In 1949 McIntosh County grocery store owner Agnes Harper built Christ's Memory Chapel on US 17, the main thoroughfare for thousands of Northerners headed for sand and sunshine. Purportedly America's smallest house of worship, leastwise in Georgia, the 10-by-15-foot chapel, with a steeple and imported stained glass, seats thirteen—just large enough, it's said, to accommodate Christ and his twelve Apostles. It's open to the public daily. Just switch off the lights as you're leaving. Take I–95 to US 17/South Newport exit.

SLOW! SAINTS CROSSING!

(Street corner sign by a Catholic school in downtown
Savannah's historic district)

The Tale of Two Valonas

Valona

Valona is a seaport in southern Albania. Valona is a fishing port in southern McIntosh County. Is there a family tie? You bet. Mrs. Lewis Graham, postmistress and conduit of vital local information at Valona's one-room United States Post Office, explained the curious link a few years ago. Her family, the Atwoods, founded the community in the 1890s as a fishing, shrimping, and oystering port. Her uncle, George Atwood, named it Shell Bluff, in honor of the oyster shells piled around the docks. "When they applied to Washington for a post office," Mrs. Graham explained, "they were told there already was a Shell Bluff, Georgia, and they had to come up with another name. Somebody looked around the docks and saw a fishing boat from Valona, Albania. They figured there couldn't be another town in Georgia, or any other place, named Valona—and there wasn't. That how we got our name."

Mrs. Graham was ninety-five when she told me that story. When she passed away a few years later, the bean-counters in Washington shut down the cozy one woman post office, and Valona, Georgia 31322 passed into history. If you'd like to see the shrimp boats a'coming and going, turn off I–95 at Eulonia, drive through Crescent, and follow the unpaved road to "downtown" Valona, population forty-five, or thereabouts.

INDEX

INDEX

INDEX

INDEX

About the Author

In the name of research, William Schemmel, whose normal diet is mainly tofu, shredded carrots, and peeled fruit, courageously engages the Luther Burger, a gastronomic A-bomb created by Mulligans Tavern, in his hometown of Decatur. "After the first bite," he reports, "long-buried lust for calories and carbs resurrected and I finished every bite, and topped off the decadence with a Fried Twinkie." For the rest of the story, see page 114. Along with this second edition of *Georgia Curiosities*, Schemmel has also written the eighth edition of *Georgia Off the Beaten Path* and the first edition of *You Know You're in Georgia When . . .*

THE INSIDER'S SOURCE

Hiking **West Virginia**

SPOOKY *South*

Off the Beaten Path **arkansas**

FLORIDA GATORS

fun WITH the Family **VIRGINIA**

NORTH CAROLINA'S MOUNTAINS

QUICK ESCAPES ATLANTA

With more than 185 South-related titles, we have the area covered. Whether you're looking for the path less traveled, a favorite place to eat, family-friendly fun, a breathtaking hike, or enchanting local attractions, our pages are filled with ideas to get you from one state to the next.

For a complete listing of all our titles, please visit our Web site at www.GlobePequot.com. The Globe Pequot Press is the largest publisher of local travel books in the United States and is a leading source for outdoor recreation guides.

FOR BOOKS TO THE SOUTH

The Globe Pequot Press

INSIDERS' GUIDE®

FALCON GUIDE®

Available wherever books are sold.
Orders can also be placed on the Web at www.GlobePequot.com,
by phone from 8:00 A.M. to 5:00 P.M. at 1-800-243-0495,
or by fax at 1-800-820-2329.